S0-AQM-488

Easy Spanish

Ben Denne and Nicole Irving

Designed by Katarina Dragoslavić
Illustrated by Ann Johns

Edited by Jane Chisholm
Series designer: Russell Punter

Language consultant: Ester Martí Marqués

Cover designed by Zoe Wray
Cover illustration by Christyan Fox

Contents

About this book

This book provides an easy introduction to the Spanish language. Each grammar page explains a particular topic, from nouns through to conditional sentences, with examples to show how Spanish is used in everyday situations. The boxes shown below highlight different learning points, and there are recommended websites that give you further opportunities to put your Spanish to the test.

This *¡Cuidado!* box means "Watch out!". It warns you of mistakes you might easily make and points out some of the differences between Spanish and English grammar.

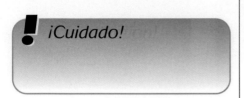

The *Learning tips* box tells you more about Spanish grammar patterns and gives you clues to help you learn them more easily.

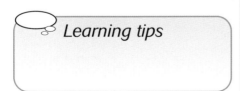

Each *Fast facts* box contains an extra gem of information. Impress your friends with your detailed knowledge of Spanish!

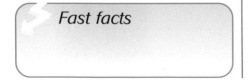

When new verbs and tenses are introduced, they are clearly presented in a verb box, with the English translation alongside.

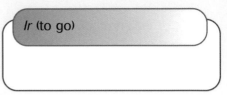

Internet links

At the Usborne Quicklinks Website we have provided links to lots of useful websites for learning Spanish.

To visit the recommended sites go to **www.usborne-quicklinks.com** and enter the keywords "**easy spanish**".

You'll find downloadable picture puzzles and links to websites with interactive quizzes, drills and exercises, pronunciation guides, online dictionaries and much more.

When using the internet, make sure you follow the safety guidelines displayed on the Usborne Quicklinks Website. The recommended sites are regularly reviewed and the links are updated, but Usborne Publishing is not responsible for the content of any website other than its own. For more information on using the internet see pages 124-125.

The Salchicha treasure: introduction

Throughout this book you can follow a story about a search for hidden treasure, using examples of the Spanish grammar you'll be learning along the way. As new words crop up, they will be listed in the *Vocabulary* box. If you need extra help, there are translations of the speech bubbles on pages 100-111.

The main characters

Fede Molinero

Carmen's brother. Likes walking, climbing, cycling and eating.

Carmen Molinero

Fede's sister. One year older than him. Likes reading crime novels.

María Salchicha

Fede and Carmen's friend. Met them whilst on holiday last year.

Alicia Salchicha

María's mother. A well-known sculptress. Runs the house on a tiny budget.

Pedro Salchicha

María's father. Son of Santiago Salchicha. Works for a charity.

Ramón Robón

A well-travelled crook. On file at Madrid headquarters.

El guardia

The local policeman. Doesn't take the three friends seriously at first.

Guau Guau

The Salchicha dog. Tireless and brave, if a bit excitable at times.

 Sometimes you will see this picture at the bottom of a page. It means there is a puzzle that needs to be solved. Look at the clues and try to figure out what Fede, Carmen and María should do next.

Understanding grammar words

Grammar is the set of rules that summarizes how a language works. It is easier to learn how Spanish works if you know a few grammar words. All the words you use when you speak or write can be split up into different types.

A **noun** is a word for a thing, an animal or a person, such as "box", "idea", "invention", "cat", or "woman". A noun is plural when you are talking about more than one, for example "boxes", "ideas" or "women".

cat

A **pronoun**, such as "he", "you", "me", "yours", is a word that stands in for a noun. If you say "The goat ate your clothes" and then, "He ate yours", you can see how "he" stands in for "goat" and "yours" stands in for "your clothes".

Is this **yours**?

An **adjective** is a word that describes something, usually a noun, for example "blue", as in "a blue jacket".

blue

Prepositions are link words such as "to", "at", "for", "near" and "under", as in "she is under the sea".

under the sea

A **verb** is an action word, such as "make", "play" or "eat", and also "have", "think" and "be". Verbs can change depending on who is doing the action, for example "I make", but "he makes". They have different **tenses** according to when the action takes place, for example "I make" but "I made". The **infinitive** form of the verb is its basic form: "to make", "to play" or "to eat". Dictionaries and word lists normally list verbs in this form.

to play football

An **adverb** is a word that gives extra information about an action. Many adverbs describe the action of a verb, for example "badly", as in "He plays tennis badly". Other adverbs describe when or where an action happens, for example "yesterday", or "here".

He plays **badly**.

Subject or object?

When used in a sentence, a noun or pronoun can have different parts to play. It is the **subject** when it is doing the action, for example "the dog" in "the dog barks" or "he" in "he barks". It is the **direct object** when it has the action done to it. For example, in the phrase "he brushes the dog", the dog is the direct object.

In the sentence "she gives money to the man", "she" is the subject, and "money" and "the man" are objects. "Money" is the direct object because it is the object that is being given. "The man" is the **indirect object** because he is receiving the direct object; it is being given **to** him.

Getting the stress right

When speaking Spanish, it is very important to stress the right part of each word. Normally, for words that end in a consonant other than *-n* or *-s*, you stress the last syllable, for example *-mir* in *dormir*. For words that end in a vowel, or *-n* or *-s*, you stress the second-to-last syllable.

Spanish words that don't follow this pattern are written with a stress mark. This shows you what part of the word to stress, for example in *árbol*. Stress marks are always placed over a vowel.

Some Spanish words have a stress mark over the part of the word you would stress anyway. This is to distinguish from another word which looks the same but has a different meaning, for example *cómo* (how) and *como* (like).

Laura passes the salad to David.
subject + verb + direct object + indirect object

Sarah drinks quietly.
subject + verb + adverb

Harry is bored.
subject + verb + adjective

Nouns

Spanish nouns are either masculine [m] or feminine [f]. These are called genders. The article (the word for "the" or "a") varies according to the gender of a noun.

Saying "the"

• The masculine word for "the" is *el*.
• The feminine word for "the" is *la*.
• The plural word for "the" is *los* for all masculine nouns.
• The plural word for "the" is *las* for all feminine nouns.

Masculine or feminine?

For a few nouns the gender is as you might expect:

e.g. *el hombre* (man) is masculine.

e.g. *la mujer* (woman) is feminine.

For most nouns, you just have to learn the gender.

el cine
(cinema)

la montaña
(mountain)

Some nouns have two forms:

la amiga [f]   *el amigo* [m]   (friend)

Saying "a" and "some"

• The masculine word for "a" is *un*.
• The feminine word for "a" is *una*.
• The masculine word for "some" is *unos*. The feminine word is *unas*.

Some examples:

un aeropuerto
(airport)

una calle (road)

un hotel (hotel)

una casa (house)

8

Making plurals

For Spanish nouns that end in a vowel, add *-s* to the end of the noun.
el castillo   -   *los castillos*
(castle)
la piscina   -   *las piscinas*
(swimming pool)

For nouns that end in a consonant, add *-es* to the end of the noun:
la ciudad   -   *las ciudades*
(town)

Learning tips

• Try to learn nouns with *el* or *la* in front of them, so that you remember their gender.

• It is usually possible to guess the gender of a noun in Spanish by looking at its ending. Nouns ending in *-o* are usually masculine. Nouns ending in *-a* are usually feminine.

el puente   el camping
el mercado   el cine   la estación
la torre   la oficina de correos   la iglesia
el castillo   la piscina
el aeropuerto   *Villatorres*

¡Cuidado! (Take care!)

In Spanish you don't always use articles as you do in English...

• When referring to a person, you use an article in Spanish where in English you don't:
e.g. *El Señor Salchicha vive en Villatorres.*
(Mr Salchicha lives in Villatorres.)

• In English, you need to use an article when stating someone's profession, but in Spanish you don't:
e.g. *Soy mecánico.*
(I'm **a** mechanic.)

• Some Spanish nouns starting with *a-* or *ha-* are feminine even though they have the article *el* instead of *la*, e.g. *el agua* (the water), *el hacha* (the axe).

The Salchicha treasure: chapter 1

Fede and his sister Carmen are flying to Villatorres from Madrid to spend a short holiday with their friend María Salchicha…

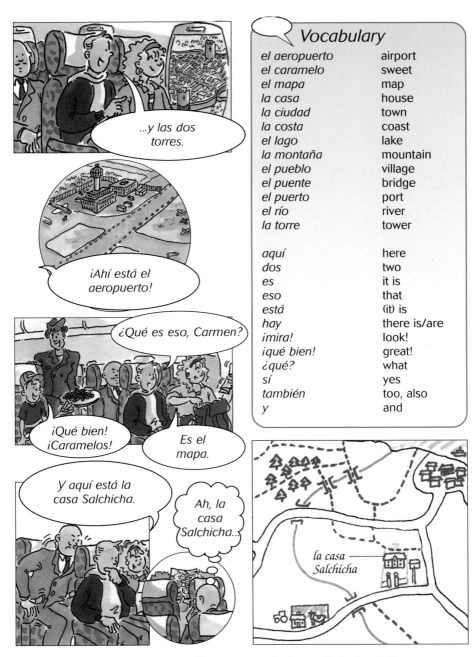

Vocabulary

el aeropuerto	airport
el caramelo	sweet
el mapa	map
la casa	house
la ciudad	town
la costa	coast
el lago	lake
la montaña	mountain
el pueblo	village
el puente	bridge
el puerto	port
el río	river
la torre	tower
aquí	here
dos	two
es	it is
eso	that
está	(it) is
hay	there is/are
¡mira!	look!
¡qué bien!	great!
¿qué?	what
sí	yes
también	too, also
y	and

As Fede and Carmen look at the map on their way in to land, the man sitting behind them is also studying it closely. He too is working out the best way to get to the Salchicha house.

Adjectives

Most Spanish adjectives come after the noun, and they sometimes change according to the gender, or if the noun is plural. This is called agreeing with the noun.

Making adjectives agree

Adjectives ending in -o already agree with masculine nouns. To make them agree with feminine nouns, you change the ending to -a. Most other adjectives do not need changing.

la maleta vieja
(the old suitcase)

la bolsa negra
(the black bag)

la tienda amarilla
(the yellow tent)

With plural nouns ending in a vowel, you add -s to the end of the adjective. With plural nouns ending in a consonant, add -es.

Before the noun?

Some Spanish adjectives come before the noun. These are:
• Adjectives of quantity.
e.g. *Mucho zumo.*
(A lot of juice.)
Poco dinero.
(A little money.)
• The adjective *grande* (big) can be used before the noun to mean "great". In this case, it is shortened to *gran*.
e.g. *Un gran jefe.*
(A great leader.)
• A few common adjectives are used before the noun in everyday expressions, but after the noun for emphasis. They are:

bueno (buen)	good
malo (mal)	bad
pequeño	small

¡Buen viaje! (Have a good journey!)

un coche rápido (a fast car)

una carretera larga (a long road)

las vacaciones perfectas
(perfect holidays)

First verbs

Spanish verbs seem more complicated than English verbs as there are lots of patterns to learn. Most verbs fall into three groups of "regular" verbs (see page 16), but there are quite a few "irregular" verbs too. These have their own unique pattern.

In Spanish, you generally use verbs without the subject pronoun. The pronoun is used for emphasis, contrast, and sometimes to be polite (see below).

Pronouns

I - *yo*
you - *tú, vosotros* or *usted*
• Use *tú* when talking to a friend, or someone your own age or younger.
• Use *vosotros* or *vosotras* [f] when talking to more than one person.
• When addressing an older person, or someone you don't know very well, use the polite form, *usted* which has the same ending as *el*. The plural is *ustedes*, which has the same ending as *ellos*.
he - *él* **she** - *ella* **it** - *él* or *ella*
• There is no word for "it", so use *él* for masculine [m] nouns and *ella* for feminine [f] nouns.
we - *nosotros* [m] / *nosotras* [f]
they - *ellos* [m] / *ellas* [f]
• When referring to a mixture of masculine and feminine things, or people, use the masculine pronoun, e.g. *ellos,* or (polite form) *ustedes.*

The verb boxes in this book do not show the less commonly used pronouns *usted, ustedes, nosotras, vosotras* and *ellas.*

la hierba verde (the green grass)

la playa es grande
(the beach is big)

Two useful irregular verbs

Querer (to want)

yo quiero	I want
tú quieres	you want
él/ella quiere	he/she/it wants
nosotros queremos	we want
vosotros queréis	you want
ellos quieren	they want

Estar (to be)

yo estoy	I am
tú estás	you are
él/ella está	he/she/it is
nosotros estamos	we are
vosotros estáis	you are
ellos están	they are

Learning tip

In the word lists of this book, irregular verbs are marked by an asterisk *.

el mar está limpio (the sea is clean)

The Salchicha treasure: chapter 2

Fede and Carmen have landed at the airport, but there seems to be some confusion in the baggage claim area. There's a real scrum at the carousel...

Hola ¿María?
Soy Carmen.

Estamos en
Villatorres.

Gracias, es usted
muy amable.

Vocabulary

el bolso	bag
la maleta	suitcase
la mochila	backpack
la salida	exit, way out
la tienda	tent
ser	to be
tener	to have
alto	tall
amable	kind, nice
azul	blue
cansado/a	tired
en	at, in
está bien	(it's) all right
éste	this
gracias	thank you
gris	grey
hola	hello
mi, mis[1]	my
negro/a	black
no	no
pequeño/a	small
perdón	sorry, excuse me
pero	but
rojo/a	red
señorita	Miss
su, sus[1]	his/hers, theirs
tu[1]	your
verde	green

[1]For more information about this kind
of adjective, go to page 21.

Está bien,
tenemos tu mapa.

Éste es tu
bolso.

No, es su bolso.

Mi mochila es
roja.

Mis maletas
son grises.

Aquí está su maleta,
señorita.

SALIDA

Making the present tense

There are three groups of Spanish verbs that follow regular patterns. They are called -AR verbs, -ER verbs and -IR verbs, because their infinitives (e.g. to walk, to choose, etc.) end in -ar, -er or -ir. To make the present tense of these verbs, you take off the -ar/-er/-ir and add a special set of endings.

-ER verbs

The infinitive of the verb "to drink" is *beber*. Take off the -er and you are left with the stem, *beb-*. Now you can add the present tense endings:

> ### Beber (to drink)
>
> | | |
> |---|---|
> | yo beb**o** | I drink |
> | tú beb**es** | you drink |
> | él/ella beb**e** | he/she/ it drinks |
> | nosotros beb**emos** | we drink |
> | vosotros beb**éis** | you drink |
> | ellos beb**en** | they drink |

-IR Verbs

-IR verbs use the same endings as -ER verbs, except for when they follow the pronouns *nosotros* and *vosotros,* where the endings become -imos and -ís. So, for example, the *nosotros / vosotros* endings for the verb *vivir* (to live, stem, *viv-*) are:
nosotros viv**imos**
vosotros viv**ís**

¡Cuidado!

In Spanish, the present tense can be used to mean the present progressive as well. So *ando* can mean either "I walk" or "I am walking".

-AR verbs

The infinitive of the verb "to speak" is *hablar*. Take off the -ar and you are left with the stem *habl-*. -AR verbs have a different set of endings from -ER verbs.

> ### Hablar (to speak)
>
> | | |
> |---|---|
> | yo habl**o** | I speak |
> | tú habl**as** | you speak |
> | él/ella habl**a** | he/she/ it speaks |
> | nosotros habl**amos** | we speak |
> | vosotros habl**áis** | you speak |
> | ellos habl**an** | they speak |

See if you can work out the endings of these regular verbs.

creer	to believe
comer	to eat
andar	to walk
buscar	to look for
dormir	to sleep

Learning tips

• Learn the endings separately, then you can add them to any regular verb.

• Some verbs have an irregular *yo* form, but the other endings are regular. Try to learn them: verbs are listed on page 112.

Ser and estar

In Spanish, there are two versions of the verb "to be". *Estar* was described on page 13. Here's the other.

Ser (to be)

yo soy	I am
tú eres	you are
él/ella es	he/she/it is
nosotros somos	we are
vosotros sois	you are
ellos son	they are

Ser or estar?

You use the verb *ser* to say what a person or thing is, or where they are from, and to describe them. You use *estar* for things that change (I'm tired, the door's open) and for saying where people and things are.

What would you like?

The Spanish for "to want" is *querer*. *Querer* is an irregular verb. You can see the endings for it on page 13.

I want to...

You can use *querer* with another verb to say what you want to do. Put the second verb in the infinitive form:
e.g. *Quiero comprar unos zapatos.* (I want to buy some shoes.)

Being polite

When you want to ask for something politely in Spanish, you use *querer* in a special tense (called the imperfect subjunctive), and say *quisiera* (I would like):
e.g. *Quisiera ir a la piscina.* (I would like to go to the swimming pool.)

¿Qué quieres hacer?
What do you want to do?

¿Qué hora es, por favor?
What time is it, please?

Quisiera comer algo.
I'd like to eat something.

Estoy buscando un hotel.
I'm looking for a hotel.

Quiero visitar un museo.
I want to visit a museum.

Vale. Vamos a un restaurante.
O.K. Let's go to a restaurant.

Espera un momento...
Wait a minute...

Fede and Carmen have managed to collect their bags from the airport and are now on their way to María's house. They stop at a café for a rest...

A man walking past Carmen drops a letter. By the time she has picked it up for him, he has driven away.

¡Oh!

Queremos alquilar unas bicicletas.

When she looks at the letter, she sees it's very strange, written to a son named Santiago and signed Sancho Salchicha...

Una isla desierta,
1893

Querido hijo Santiago,

Soy un hombre viejo. Estoy solo en un isla desierta y mi casa cerca de Villatorres está vacía. Tengo un secreto. Soy muy rico.

Ahora mi tesoro es tu tesoro. Mi casa oculta la primera pista. En primer lugar busca los dos barcos.

Adiós,

Sancho Salchicha

Vocabulary

el barco	boat, ship
la bicicleta	bike
el hijo	son
el hombre	man
la manzana	apple
la mesa	table
la naranja	orange
el paisaje	countryside
el pájaro	bird
la pista	clue
el secreto	secret
el sol	sun
el tesoro	treasure
el zumo	juice
alquilar	to rent
brillar	to shine
cantar	to sing
hacer*	to do/make
ocultar	to hide
pagar	to pay
querer*	to want
ver*	to see/look at
visitar	to visit
adiós	farewell
ahora	now
a la sombra	in the shade
desierto/a	deserted
despacio	slowly
dos	two
en primer lugar	first of all
fácil	easy
frío/a	cold
lento/a	slowly
por favor	please
primero/a	first
querido/a	dear
rico/a	rich
solo/a	alone, only
todo recto	straight ahead

*Remember, an asterisk (*) means the verb is irregular.

Whose is it?

In Spanish, to say that something belongs to someone, you use *de* (of). So "Fede's sweater" is, word for word, "the sweater of Fede" - *el jersey de Fede*. In answer to *¿De quién es?* (Whose is it?), you say *Es de Fede* (It's Fede's), or simply *De Fede* (Fede's).

Using *de* with nouns

When you use *de* with a feminine or plural noun, such as "the girl", you just add *la chica*. So "the girl's boots" is *las botas de la chica*.

With masculine singular nouns, *de* and *el* join together to make the word *del*. So "the boy's shoes" would be *los zapatos del chico*.

This and these

The Spanish for "this" is *este* (plural *estos*) for masculine nouns, and *esta* (plural *estas*) for feminine nouns: e.g. *Este billete es de Pedro.* (This ticket is Pedro's.) *Esta ropa son de Carmen.* (These clothes are Carmen's.)

Learning tip

Esto ("this") is a neutral pronoun used to describe situations: e.g. *Esto no me gusto nada.* (I don't like this at all.)

That

There are two words for "that" in Spanish: *ese* and *aquel*. The feminine forms are *esa* and *aquella*. The plurals are *esos* [m] / *esas* [f] and *aquellos* [m] / *aquellas* [f] You use *ese* when talking about something nearby, and *aquel* when talking about something far away.

Tener (to have)

yo tengo	I have
tú tienes	you have
él/ella tiene	he/she/ it has
nosotros tenemos	we have
vosotros tenéis	you have
ellos tienen	they have

Have and have to

The verb "to have" in Spanish is *tener* (see above). If it is used with *que*, its meaning changes to "have to" (must): e.g. *Tengo una camisa verde.* (I have a green shirt.) *Tengo que ir a la escuela.* (I have to (must) go to school.)

Fast Facts

The verb "to have" can also be translated as *haber*. See page 56 for more about this.

My, your, his, her...

To say things like "my skirt" or "your house" in Spanish, you have to use a special kind of adjective. The adjective must agree with the noun it refers to. Here are the different forms. Where the masculine and feminine endings are different, the endings are shown in bold:

	[m]/[f]	**[pl]**
my	*mi*	*mis*
your	*tu*	*tus*
his/her/ its	*su*	*sus*
our	*nuestro/a*	*nuestros/as*
your	*vuestro/a*	*vuestros/as*
their	*su*	*sus*

Llevamos nuestra ropa nueva.
We're wearing our new clothes.

La ropa

las botas	boots
el calcetín	sock
la camisa	shirt
la camiseta	T-shirt
el chándal	track suit
la chaqueta	jacket
el cinturón	belt
la falda	skirt
el jersey	sweater
las medias	tights
los pantalones	trousers
los pantalones cortos	shorts
la ropa	clothes
el sombrero	hat
la sudadera	sweatshirt
el traje	suit
los vaqueros	jeans
las zapatillas de deporte	trainers
el zapato	shoe
gustar (see p. 31)	to like
llevar	to wear, carry

mi camiseta

mi jersey

mi camisa

mis vaqueros

mis pantalones

mis zapatillas de deporte

mis zapatos

Fede and Carmen arrive at the Salchicha house where they are shown lots of interesting things and meet a very destructive goat in the garden. How silly of them to leave their bags on the steps outside...

¡Buenos días! Somos los amigos de María.

¡Buenos días! Yo soy su madre.

Me llamo Alicia... y este es nuestro perro Guau Guau.

¿De quién es el gato?

Es de María. Se llama Kiti.

Aquí está la habitación de mis padres...

...mi habitación y...

...la habitación del huésped.

Aquí escondemos todos los tesoros de la familia.

Aquí está el estudio de mi madre.

Y ese es un retrato antiguo del abuelo de María, Santiago.

Ese es un cuadro muy viejo de la casa Salchicha.

¡Oh, no! Es Comelotodo, la cabra de los vecinos. ¡Come cualquier cosa!

Vocabulary

el/la *abuelo/a*	grandfather/ grandmother
el/la *amigo/a*	friend
la *cabra*	goat
el *cuadro*	painting
el *estudio*	studio
las *gafas*	glasses
el *gato*	cat
la *habitación*	(bed)room
el/la *hermano/a*	brother/sister
el *huésped*	lodger
la *madre*	mother
los *padres*	parents
el *perro*	dog
los *prismáticos*	binoculars
el *retrato*	portrait
el/la *vecino/a*	neighbour
esconder	to hide
llamarse	to be called
¿de quién?	whose?
buenos días	good morning
antiguo/a	ancient/old

¿De quién es esa ropa?

Es de mi hermano.

¿Y estos prismáticos?

Son también de Fede.

Me gustan estas gafas.

Son de Carmen.

Telling people what to do

There are several ways to tell someone what to do in Spanish. You can use the imperative of the verb (Wait! Go! Stop!), or you can use "must" or "have to", as in "you must tidy your room".

Making the imperative

There are two main forms of the imperative in Spanish. You can make it with the *tú* form of a verb by removing the *-s*. You can also make it with the *vosotros* form of a verb by replacing the *-r* of the verb's infinitive with *-d*.

Andáis becomes *¡Andad!* (walk!)

Saying must

Deber (to have to, must) is a useful verb for saying what you must do. It is always used with the infinitive of another verb.
e.g. *Debo ir al banco.*
(I must go to the bank).

Deber (to have to, must)

yo deb**o**	I must
tú deb**es**	you must
él/ella deb**e**	he/she/ it must
nosotros deb**emos**	we must
vosotros deb**éis**	you must
ellos deb**en**	they must

Irregular imperatives

Some irregular verbs have a *tú* form which does not follow the pattern described above, but the *vosotros* form is regular.

verb	*tú* form	translation
decir	di	say
hacer	haz	make
ir	ve	go
poner	pon	put
salir	sal	go out
ser	sé	be
tener	ten	have
venir	ven	come

Debes comprar esto.
You must buy this.

Fast facts

The imperative is never used for negatives in Spanish, so while you would say *¡habla!* (speak!), you would never say *¡no habla!* (don't speak!).

24

Giving directions

The imperative is very useful for giving and understanding directions. Here is a list of direction words:

la calle	street
el camino	path, lane, way
la carretera (principal)	(main) road
la intersección	junction
el paso de peatones	pedestrian crossing
la plaza	square
semáforo	traffic light
continuar	to carry on
cruzar	to cross
girar	to turn
ir*	to go
seguir	to follow
tomar	to take
venir*	to come
primero/a	first
segundo/a	second
tercero/a	third
cuarto/a	fourth
todo recto	straight ahead
a la izquierda	(to/on the) left
a la derecha	(to/on the) right

Using *hay que*

The verb *haber* (there is/are) is sometimes used with *que* as an imperative in the third person form (*hay*). It is always used with the infinitive of another verb, and translates as "it is necessary":
e.g. *Hay que limpiar la casa*.
(It is necessary to clean the house.)

Hay que reservar. It is necessary to book.

¡Cuidado!

Some verbs, called reflexive verbs (see page 44), need an extra pronoun. In the imperative form, the reflexive pronoun goes on the end of the word:
e.g. *Te levantas.*
(You get up.)
¡Levántate!
(Get up!)

¡Juguemos al fútbol!
Let's play football!

¡Pásalo aquí! Pass it here!

A la izquierda. To the left.

¡Tenemos que ganar! We must win!

The Salchicha treasure: chapter 5

The three friends are doing battle with Comelotodo, the neighbour's goat.
They're having a tough time getting the animal back where it belongs.

That chore done, the three friends decide to visit an old church nearby.
They go off on their bicycles, leaving the house unattended...

Unknown to them, an unwelcome visitor arrives.

Ésta debe de ser la casa Salchicha.

Hay que encontrar esa pista rápidamente.

En primer lugar tengo que buscar mi lima.

¡Cállate!

Estas cerraduras deben de ser muy viejas.

Vocabulary

la barrera	gate
la cerradura	lock
la corda	rope
la cueva	cave
la iglesia	the church
la lima	nail file
la pista	clue
callarse	to be quiet
cerrar	to close, to shut
cuidarse	to watch out, to be careful
encontrar	to find
girar	to turn
hacer compras	to do some shopping
lanzar	to throw
tirar	to pull
tomar	to take
visitar	to visit
antiguo/a	antique
aquí	here
bueno/a	good, OK
date prisa	hurry up
despacio	slowly
ésta	this one
hasta luego	see you later
rápidamente	quickly, fast
rápido/a	quick
todo/a	everything
tranquilo/a	quiet, calm
viejo/a	old

Asking questions

There are two different ways to ask questions in Spanish, and there are many question words - such as when, where, why - that can be added to the sentence.

Add question marks

One way to ask a question is to change the tone of your voice. To show this in writing, you put a question mark (?) after the sentence and an upside-down question mark before it.

¿Tienes bocadillos?
Do you have any sandwiches?

Make an inversion

You can turn a sentence into a question by putting the subject after the verb. This is called an inversion. When the sentence is a statement, the order is subject + verb. With an inversion, this becomes verb + subject. So *Fede tiene una hermana* (Fede has a sister) becomes *¿Tiene Fede una hermana?* (Does Fede have a sister?)

Who's it about?

Because pronouns are often left out in Spanish, you need to look at the verb ending to find out who the question is about:

e.g. *¿Quieres ir al cine?*
(Do **you** want to go to the cinema?)

Question words

¿cómo?	how?
¿cuándo?	when
¿cuál?	which one?
¿cuánto/a?	how much/many?
¿dónde?	where?
¿por qué?	why?
¿qué?	what?, which?
¿quién(es)	who?

Cuánto changes like an adjective to agree with the noun that follows. The feminine version of *cuánto* is *cuánta,* and the plural is *cuántos* [m] or *cuántas* [f]:
e.g. *¿Cuántos hermanos tienes?* (How many brothers do you have?)

¿Cuándo sale el tren?
When does the train leave?

¿Porqué sale con retraso?
Why is it late?

How to use question words

Question words go at the beginning of the sentence in Spanish. So, to ask "Where are you?", you would use the question word, followed by the verb: *¿Dónde estás?*
If you are including the subject noun, you would put it at the end:
e.g. *¿Dónde está Fede?*
(Where is Fede?)

Can I? May I?

The Spanish verb *poder* can be translated as "to be able to", "can" or "may". You often use this irregular verb with another verb in the infinitive to ask permission to do something.
e.g. *¿Puedo comprar esto?*
(Can/May I buy this?)
Be careful to include the question marks. Without them, the above would mean "I can buy this."

Poder (can, may)

yo puedo	I can
tú puedes	you can
él/ella puede	he/she/it can
nosotros podemos	we can
vosotros podéis	you can
ellos pueden	they can

Poder is also used with *que* to mean "might".
e.g. *Puede que la situación mejore.*
(The situation might improve.)

Fast facts

• *Qué* + noun can also be used in exclamations:
e.g. *¡Qué sorpresa!*
(What a surprise!)
¡Qué mala suerte!
(What bad luck!)

¿Qué desea?

la cesta	basket
la farmacia	pharmacy
la fresa	strawberry
el helado	ice-cream
el kilo (followed by *de* + noun)	kilo (of)
la manzana	apple
la naranja	orange
la panadería	baker's
el pastel	cake
el sabor	flavour
el supermercado	supermarket
comprar	to buy
costar	to cost
explicar	to explain
llevar	to carry, to wear
probar	to try/taste
vender	to sell

¿Cuánto valen estos zapatos?
How much do these shoes cost?

¿Puedo ver esa camiseta?
May I see that t-shirt?

María's mother, Alicia, is doing her grocery shopping...

Meanwhile, Fede, Carmen and María have arrived at the church. While they're resting, Carmen remembers the letter that the man dropped at the café...

María knows that Sancho was her great-grandfather. After studying his letter to his son Santiago, she realizes that it is the start of a trail of clues leading to hidden treasure.

First they will need to go back to the house to look at the two old pictures of ships...

Vocabulary

la broma	joke
la búsqueda del tesoro	treasure hunt
el cangrejo	crab
la carta	letter
la farmacia	pharmacy
el Mago	magician
abrir	to open
explicar	to explain
probar	to try, taste
enfermo/a	ill
de verdad	real, true

Negatives

You make a sentence negative in Spanish by putting the word *no* (meaning "not" or "no") into the sentence. This usually comes just before the verb, so *yo no quiero comer* means "I don't want to eat". Notice how, unlike English where you add the verb "do", you don't need an extra verb to make this sentence negative in Spanish.

Useful negative words

These words can all be used before a verb, to make a negative sentence:

no	not/no
nada	nothing
nadie	nobody
nunca	never
tampoco	neither

e.g. *Yo tampoco*
(Me neither)

Lo siento, pero **no** puedo repararla.
I'm sorry but I can't repair it.

There aren't any...

In Spanish you don't normally use a word for "any"- you use *no hay*.
e.g. *No hay libros.*
(There aren't any books.)
However, *ningún* (feminine *ninguna*) is used to stress that there are none **at all**. It is always singular:
e.g. *No tengo ningún libro.*
(I haven't got any books at all.)

None and any

Most negative words in Spanish can be placed before or after the verb in a sentence. If you put them after the verb, you put the word *no* before the verb and their meaning changes slightly:

	with *no*
nada	(not) anything
nadie	(not) anybody
nunca	(not) ever
tampoco	(not) either

e.g. *Nunca está enfermo.*
(He's never ill.)
No está enfermo nunca.
(He's never ill, ever.)

¡Nadie comprende nada!
Nobody understands anything!

Learning tips

In English, two negatives cancel each other out. This doesn't always happen in Spanish:
e.g. *No tengo ningún libro.*
I don't have any books (not "I don't have no books").

Saying that you know

Spanish uses two different verbs to talk about what and who you know. To say that you know how to do something (e.g. I know how to swim), you use *saber*. To say that you know, or are acquainted with, someone or somewhere, you use *conocer*. Both verbs are irregular.

Saber (to know, to know how to)

yo sé	I know
tú sabes	you know
él/ella sabe	he/she/it knows
nosotros sabemos	we know
vosotros sabéis	you know
ellos saben	they know

⚡ *Fast facts*

• Notice that both *saber* and *conocer* have irregular endings in the first person.
Other examples of verbs with irregular *yo* endings are:
hacer (to make): *yo hago*
poner (to put): *yo pongo*
traer (to bring): *yo traigo*

Conocer (to know, to be acquainted with)

yo conozco	I know
tú conoces	you know
él/ella conocen	he/she/it knows
nosotros conocemos	we know
vosotros conocéis	you know
ellos conocen	they know

Things you like

In Spanish, to say you like something you use the verb *gustar*. This translates as "to please". It is used with a special kind of pronoun, called an object pronoun, which goes before the verb. When you say you like something in Spanish, you actually say "it pleases me".

pronoun	object pronoun
yo	me
tú	te
él/ella	le
nosotros	nos
vosotros	os
ellos/ellas	les

e.g. *Me gusta la leche.*
("I like milk", or "milk pleases me".)

¿Quién gana?
Who's winning?

No sé.
I don't know.

¡No es posible!
That's not possible!

The Salchicha treasure: chapter 7

Alicia arrives home with her groceries. She starts cooking without realizing there's someone in the house or, to be more precise, someone in her studio...

La puerta no está cerrada con llave.

Pero las bicicletas no están ahí...

¡Silencio, Guau Guau! No hay que ladrar tan fuerte.

¿Qué buscas?

No hay nadie.

¡Hay un ladrón en la casa!

¿Qué barcos? No veo ningun barco.

¡Buenas noches, Pedro! ¡Hola Juan!

Buenas noches, Alicia. ¡Oh no! No hay ninguna aspirina.

Sí, ya lo sé. La farmacia está cerrada.

No tengo nada, no tengo aspirinas, no tengo esparadrapo...

María, Fede and Carmen arrive home and head straight for the studio and the two paintings. The burglar makes a hasty retreat...

¡Hola a todo el mundo!

Aquí están los dos barcos.

¡Oh, no!, y aún no tengo la pista.

¡Ay va! Hay un hombre afuera.

María, ¿quién es ese hombre?

No sé.

No es Juan, el huésped...

¿Dónde estábais? La cena está lista.

¡Mirad! No son exactamente iguales.

Vale, mamá. Un momento.

Vocabulary

la aspirina	aspirin
el esparadrapo	adhesive bandage
el huésped	lodger
el ladrón	burglar
la puerta	door
ladrar	to bark
mirar	to look
traer	to bring
afuera	outside
buenas noches	good evening/ good night
cena	supper
cerrado/a con llave	locked
en	in
exactamente	exactly
fuerte	loud(ly)
igual	(the) same
nada	nothing
niguno	no, none, nothing
listo/a	ready
pero	but
porque	because
¡silencio!	silence!
tan	so
todo el mundo	everybody
vale	OK, fine
ya lo sé	I know

The first clue

Six missing items in the second picture are enough to tell the three friends where the next clue must be. They decide to go there the next day.

Picture one

Picture two

Can you spot which six items are missing in the second picture?
(The same items have already appeared in the story, on a sign over a door...)

35

Stem-changing verbs

In Spanish, there is a small group of verbs called stem-changing verbs. These are verbs which have a change in their stem (the bit before -ar, -er or -ir). However, unlike other irregular verbs, they have regular endings.

Changing the stem

In stem-changing verbs, the change occurs in all but the *nosotros* and *vosotros* forms of the verb. It is always a vowel change within the stem of the verb: *e* changes to *ie* or *i*, and *o* and *u* change to *ue*.

Pensar (to think)

yo *pienso*	I think
tú *piensas*	you think
él/ella *piensa*	he/she/it thinks
nosotros *pensamos*	we think
vosotros *pensáis*	you think
ellos *piensan*	they think

In the above example, *pensar* has an *e* in the stem. It is a stem-changing verb, so the original stem *pen-* changes to *pien-*. The endings themselves are the same as for any -ar verb.

¿Y tú, qué piensas?
What do you think?

O and u stems

In these verbs, the stem vowel changes to *ue*, as in *volver*, shown below. The endings remain regular.

Volver (to return/to come)

yo *vuelvo*	I return
tú *vuelves*	you return
él/ella *vuelve*	he/she/it returns
nosotros *volvemos*	we return
vosotros *volvéis*	you return
ellos *vuelven*	they return

¡Volvemos a la casa!
We're going back home!

Other stem-changing verbs

costar (stem *cuest-*)	to cost
dormir (stem *duerm-*)	to sleep
encontrar (stem *encuentr-*)	to meet/find
jugar (stem *jueg-*)	to play
morir (stem *muer-*)	to die
probar (stem *prueb-*)	to try/taste
recordar (stem *recuerd-*)	to remember
soñar (stem *sueñ-*)	to dream

E stems

Stem-changing verbs that have an *e* in their stem change to either *i* or *ie*, depending on the verb. There is no rule for this change, so you have to learn each verb separately. Here are some useful ones:

cerrar (stem *cierr-*)   to shut
servir (stem *sirv-*)   to serve
pedir (stem *pid-*)   to order
preferir (stem *prefier-*)   to prefer

Pedir (to order/ask for)

yo pido	I order
tú pides	you order
él/ella pide	he/she/it orders
nosotros pedimos	we order
vosotros pedís	you order
ellos piden	they order

Fast facts

Stem-changing verbs in this book are introduced with a bracketed *ie*, *i* or *ue* next to them, showing you what the stem vowel changes to.

Losing and missing

The Spanish stem-changing verb *perder* means "to lose", but it can also mean "to miss":
e.g. *No quieren perder el autobús.* (They don't want to miss the bus.)

Smells different

The verb *oler* (to smell) is stem-changing, but you also add an *h-* to the beginning, to make the stem *huel*.

Oler (to smell)

yo huelo	I smell
tú hueles	you smell
él/ella huele	he/she/it smells
nosotros olemos	we smell
vosotros oléis	you smell
ellos huelen	they smell

Algo huele mal por aquí.
Something smells bad here.

¡Espero que no sea nuestra comida!
I hope it's not our food!

37

The Salchicha treasure: chapter 8

The next day, Fede, Carmen and María have arrived at the *Magician's Inn*, in search of the next clue. María has her camera with her. But finding what they're looking for isn't easy with all those people around, and unknown to the three friends they are being watched...

Vamos al supermercado, cariño.

¡Silencio! Estoy leyendo el periódico.

¿A qué hora empieza la película?

¿A qué hora vuelve a casa esta noche?

¡Qué bien huele!

Vocabulary

la ensalada	salad
el filete	steak
la foto	photo
la hamburguesa	hamburger
el niño	child, boy
la noche	evening/night
las patatas fritas	chips, French fries
la película	film
el periódico	newspaper
el queso	cheese
la sopa	soup
el supermercado	supermarket
empezar (ie)	to start
leer	to read
oler (hue)	to smell
pedir (i)	to order
preferir (ie)	to prefer
sacar fotos	to take photos
salir	to leave
volver (ue)	to return
ahora mismo	straight, right away, this instant.
hoy	today
mal	bad
otro/a	other
pronto	soon, early
próximo/a	next
ya basta	that's enough

Prepositions

Prepositions are words like "in", "on" or "of". Most Spanish prepositions are easy to use. For example: *Tu jersey está en tu habitación.* (Your sweater is in your room.)

Common prepositions

a	to, at (for time)
al lado de	by, next to
antes de	before
cerca de	close to, near
con	with
contra	against
de	of, from, by
debajo de	under, underneath
delante de	in front of
dentro de	inside
desde	from, since
detrás de	behind
en	in, at, on
encima de	on, over
enfrente de	opposite
entre	between, among
fuera de	outside
hacia	toward, about
hasta	until
junto a	next to
lejos de	far from
para	for, toward, to
por	for (because of), through, along
según	according to
sin	without
sobre	over, on top of
tras	after

Prepositions and places

In Spanish, to say "from" and "to" you normally use *de* and *a*:
e.g. *Soy de España.*
(I come **from** Spain.)
Voy a Madrid.
(I'm going **to** Madrid.)

To say that you are **in** a certain country, you use *en*:
e.g. *Estoy en Italia.*
(I'm **in** Italy.)
En is also used when talking about transport (see *¡Cuidado!* box).

For people, you always use the preposition *a*:
e.g. *Quiero visitar a mis padres.*
(I want to visit my parents.)

Quiero ir a Quito.
I want to go to Quito.

¡Cuidado!

In Spanish you don't always use the same preposition as in English:
e.g. *Estoy en el tren.*
(I'm **on** the train.)
Voy a Madrid en tren.
(I'm going to Madrid **by** train.)

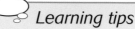

Learning tips

If *de* or *a* come before *el*, they are shortened to **del** and **al**.
e.g. *Fuera del café.*
(Outside the café.)
Quiero ir al cine.
(I want to go to the cinema.)

Where do you live?

The Spanish verb *vivir* means "to live". It is a regular verb:
e.g. *¿Dónde vives?*
(Where do you live?)

To ask where somebody is from, you use the verb *ser*.
e.g. *¿De dónde eres?*
(Where are you from?)

Prepositions and verbs

Some Spanish verbs need a preposition after them when followed by another verb. Here are some useful ones to remember:

aprender a	to learn to
dejar de	to fail to
olvidarse de	to forget to
tratar de	to try to
insistir en	to insist on

If you need to use a verb after a preposition in Spanish, you always put it in the infinitive form:
e.g. *Aprendo a hablar Espanol.*
(I am learning to speak Spanish.)
Insisto en pagar la cuenta.
(I insist on paying the bill.)

Some country names

Alemania	Germany
Australia	Australia
Austria	Austria
Escocia	Scotland
España	Spain
Estados Unidos	United States
Francia	France
Inglaterra	England
Irlanda	Ireland
Italia	Italy
Japón	Japan
Portugal	Portugal

The continents

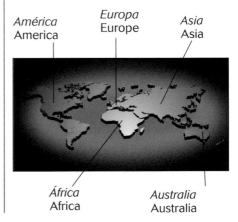

América
America

Europa
Europe

Asia
Asia

África
Africa

Australia
Australia

Dos amigas están sentades en la playa junto del mar.
Two friends are sitting on the beach next to the sea.

Carmen está debajo de la sombrilla.
Carmen is under the parasol.

María está al lado de ella.
María is next to her.

41

The Salchicha treasure: chapter 9

Outside the inn, Carmen spots the man who has been following them. He is on his way out. Fede, Carmen and María realize they have seen him before. He too must be after the treasure.

They have to lose him quickly, so they head for the harbour.

Podemos ir a casa de mi amigo, Rafa. Vive enfrente de la estación.

Sí, tengo una lupa. Está encima de la mesa en el desván.

Vocabulary

el/la amig**o/a**	friend
el árbol	tree
el banco	bench, bank
el colegio	school
la colina	hill
el desván	attic
el edificio	building
la fuente	fountain
el jardín	garden
la lupa	magnifying glass
el muelle	quay, dock
la mujer	woman
la nota	note
la pregunta	question
la red	net
la respuesta	answer
la salida	exit
la vaca	cow
la ventana	window
poder	to be able to, can
vivir	to live
allí	(over) there
bien	good, right, OK
calv**o/a**	bald

Using the magnifying glass, Fede, María and Carmen look at the note that Fede found at the inn. At first it is very puzzling, but with the help of María's photograph of the painted seat at the inn, they work out where to go next.

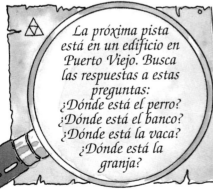

La próxima pista está en un edificio en Puerto Viejo. Busca las respuestas a estas preguntas:
¿Dónde está el perro?
¿Dónde está el banco?
¿Dónde está la vaca?
¿Dónde está la granja?

Can you figure out where the three friends must go next?
(Try and find a building on this page which matches the answers to Sancho Salchicha's questions. The first answer is *debajo del árbol*.)

43

Reflexive verbs

Reflexive verbs are verbs which include a pronoun, such as *me* (myself) and *te* (yourself). The pronoun "reflects back" the subject of the verb, which means that the subject and the object are the same, e.g. *yo me levanto* (I get myself up).

Forming reflexive verbs

Spanish reflexive verbs follow patterns just like ordinary verbs, except that there is a pronoun between the subject and the verb. The pronouns are:

me	myself
te	yourself
se	himself, herself, itself
nos	ourselves
os	yourselves
se	themselves

Note that Spanish reflexive verbs always have a reflexive pronoun with them, while in English the reflexive pronoun is optional: e.g. *levantarse* (to get up):

Lavarse (to wash)

yo me lavo	I wash (myself)
tú te lavas	you wash (yourself)
él/ella se lava	he/she washes (himself/herself)
nosotros nos lavamos	we wash (ourselves)
vosotros os laváis	you wash (yourselves)
ellos se lavan	they wash (themselves)

Useful reflexive verbs

acostarse (ue)	to go to bed
bañarse	to take a bath
calmarse	to calm down
cambiarse	to get changed
casarse	to get married
defenderse	to defend oneself
despedirse (i)	to take leave
despertarse (ie)	to wake up
dormirse (ue)	to fall asleep
ducharse	to take a shower
encenderse (ie)	to catch fire
encontrarse (ue)	to be found/situated
irse*	to leave
lavarse	to wash oneself
levantarse	to get up
llamarse	to be called
llevarse	to take away/carry
ponerse*	to put on
quedarse	to remain
quitarse	to take off (clothing)
sentirse (ie)	to sit down
vestirse (i)	to dress
volverse (ue)	to turn

Giving orders

In the *tú* form, reflexive verbs make their imperatives in the same way as ordinary verbs. But, the pronoun (*te*) comes after the verb as part of the same word, e.g. *¡levántate!* (get up!) To make imperatives of reflexive verbs using *vosotros*, remove the -*d* from the ending of the verb's imperative and add -*os*: e.g. *sentaos* (sit down).

Fast facts

• The infinitive of reflexive verbs always ends with *-se*.

• Lots of verbs have both a normal and a reflexive form. Use the reflexive form if the subject and object of the phrase or sentence are the same.

Using negatives

To use a reflexive verb in the negative, you put *no* before the pronoun and the subject.

No me levanto.
I'm not getting up.

Spot the difference

With reflexive verbs, the subject and object are the same:
e.g. *Yo me lavo (lavarse).*
(I wash myself.)
With ordinary verbs, the subject and object are different:
e.g. *Yo lavo el coche (lavar).*
(I wash the car.)

Who and which

In Spanish, you usually use *que* for "who" "whom" and "which". *Que* can refer to either the subject or the object, so you say *la chica/el libro **que** esta allí* (the girl/book over there) and *la chica/el libro **que** busco* (the girl/book I'm looking for). *Que* is never left out, although "who" and "which" are often left out in English.

After a preposition though, you use *quien* to refer to a person and *quienes* (the plural) to refer to people:
e.g. *la chica con **quien** hablo* (the girl who I'm talking to/the girl with whom I'm talking).

Telling the time

To answer *¿Qué hora es?* (What time is it?), you say *es la* (singular) for one-o-clock or midnight/midday, or *son las…*(pl) for all other times:

Es mediodia/medianoche

Es la una menos cuarto

Son las diez menos veinte

Son las diez y media

Son las once y cuarto

Son las tres

Fede, Carmen and María are at the school, looking for the next clue. They creep past the classrooms where different lessons are going on. Unknown to the three friends, they are still being followed...

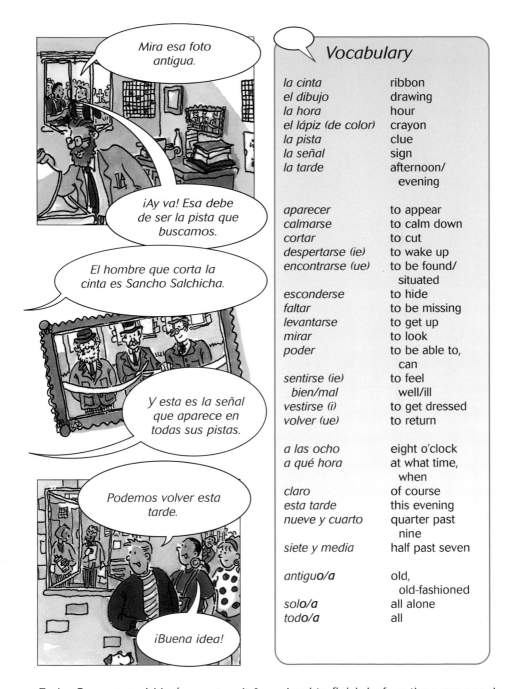

Vocabulary

la cinta	ribbon
el dibujo	drawing
la hora	hour
el lápiz (de color)	crayon
la pista	clue
la señal	sign
la tarde	afternoon/ evening
aparecer	to appear
calmarse	to calm down
cortar	to cut
despertarse (ie)	to wake up
encontrarse (ue)	to be found/ situated
esconderse	to hide
faltar	to be missing
levantarse	to get up
mirar	to look
poder	to be able to, can
sentirse (ie) bien/mal	to feel well/ill
vestirse (i)	to get dressed
volver (ue)	to return
a las ocho	eight o'clock
a qué hora	at what time, when
claro	of course
esta tarde	this evening
nueve y cuarto	quarter past nine
siete y media	half past seven
antiguo/a	old, old-fashioned
solo/a	all alone
todo/a	all

Fede, Carmen and María must wait for school to finish before they can sneak back to look at the old photograph.

Saying what you're doing

*H*acer is a common Spanish verb which means "to do" or "to make". It has many different uses, including describing the weather (e.g. *hace frío* - it's cold) and talking about an action (e.g. *hacer gimnasia* - to do gymnastics).

Hacer (to do, to make)

yo hago	I make
tú haces	you make
él/ella hace	he/she/it makes
nosotros hacemos	we make
vosotros hacéis	you make
ellos hacen	they make

¿Qué haces esta tarde?
What are you doing this evening?

Uses of *hacer*

hace una hora...	it's been an hour...
hace dos meses	two months ago
hace mal tiempo	the weather's bad

It happened yesterday...

Hacer is also used when talking about time, to mean "ago".

e.g. *Hace unas semanas.*
(A few weeks ago.)

Talking about the weather

Often *hacer* is used with an adjective or a noun to describe the weather. To ask about the weather you say:
¿Qué tiempo hace?
(What's the weather like?)

Hace buen tiempo.
It's fine.

Hace calor.
It's hot.

Hace frío.
It's cold.

Hace viento.
It's windy.

In the middle of...

You can use the present progressive tense to emphasise that you are in the middle of doing something. Use *estar*, followed by a special form of the verb describing what you are doing. To make this form, add *-ando* to the stem of *-ar* verbs, and *-iendo* to the stem of *-ir* and *-er* verbs:
e.g. *Estoy comiendo.*
(I am eating.)

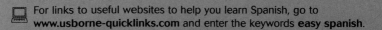
Saying because

Porque means "because" in Spanish.
e.g. *No quiero salir **porque** hace frío.*
(I don't want to go out **because** it's cold.)
It can also be split into two words (*por qué*), to mean "**why**".
To say "because of", you use *por*.
e.g. *Estoy aquí **por** María.*
I'm here **because of** María.

Using *para*

Para can mean "for" (see page 40), but it is also used with a verb in the infinitive to mean "in order to", "so as to", or "to".

e.g. *Van a la playa **para** tomar el sol.*
(They go to the beach **in order to** sunbathe.)

Other uses of *por* and *para*

You can use *por* to ask questions.
e.g. *¿**Por** dónde?*
(Which way?)

Para quien means "**for whom**", and *para que* means "**for which**".

¡No puedo dormir por el ruido!
I can't sleep because of the noise!

¡Yo también! Me gusto mucho esquiar en los Alpes.
Me too! I like skiing in the Alps.

¡Estoy contenta porque hay mucha nieve!
I'm happy because there's a lot of snow!

49

The Salchicha treasure: chapter 11

Before Fede, Carmen and María return to the school, the bald man pulls off a neat bit of impersonation and gets away with the photo...

Porque ése es su maletín.

Bien, debemos ir a la comisaría.

Vocabulary

la comisaría	police station
la fotocopiadora	photocopier
el maletín	briefcase
la pieza	part
el policía	policeman
el técnico	mechanic
arreglar	to repair, to mend
cerrar	to close, to shut
entrar	to enter, to go in
envolver (ue)	to wrap (up)
bastante	quite, enough
ese/a	that (one)
mañana por la mañana	tomorrow morning
roto/a	broken
simpático	nice
tonto/a	silly

Outside the police station...

Está cerrada.

Bueno, tendremos que volver mañana por la mañana.

¿Conoces al policía?

Sí, es bastante simpático.

51

Personal pronouns

A personal pronoun is a short word that replaces the noun, such as "he" instead of "John", and "it" instead of "the car". *Yo, tú, él/ella, nosotros, vosotros* and *ellos* are called subject pronouns, because they replace the subject of the sentence. Object pronouns are words like "him", "her" and "them", which replace the object of the sentence. In the sentence "I buy them", "I" is the subject pronoun and "them" is the object pronoun.

Direct object pronouns

Object pronouns can either be direct or indirect. You use a direct object pronoun when you are replacing a noun which is the direct object of a sentence.

For instance, in the sentence *Pedro come el helado*, you can replace *el helado* with **lo**. The object pronoun always goes immediately before the verb, so *Pedro come el helado* becomes *Pedro lo come*.

Pedro lo come. (Pedro is eating it.)

Here is a list of direct object pronouns:

me	me
te	you
lo	him/it
la	her/it
nos	us
os	you
los/las	them [m]/[f]

With a negative, the pronoun still comes immediately before the verb:
e.g. *Pedro **no lo** come.*
(Pedro **isn't** eating **it**.)

Indirect object pronouns

If the object in a sentence can be preceded by the word "to", then it is known as indirect. So, in the sentence "I speak to Pedro", the indirect object is "Pedro". The indirect object can be replaced by a different kind of pronoun, called an indirect object pronoun. The indirect object pronouns are:

me	(to) me
te	(to) you
le	(to) him/her/it
nos	(to) us
os	(to) you
les	(to) them

So, for example, the sentence *Le hablo **a Pedro*** can be shortened to *Le hablo*.

Pronouns after prepositions

Sometimes you need to use a preposition (a word like "in", "on" or "for" - see page 40) with a personal pronoun after it. In most cases you use the subject pronoun (*el/nosotros* etc):
e.g. *Eso es **para él**.*
(This is **for him**.)
There are a couple of exceptions. *Mí* replaces *yo* and *ti* replaces *tú*:
e.g. *La linterna es **para mí**.*
(The torch is **for me**.)
*Esas cosas son **para ti**.*
(These things are **for you**.)

Word order

Spanish personal pronouns usually go before the verb. But in the present progressive tense they can also go on the end of the *-ndo* form: e.g. *Está mirándome*.
(He's watching me.)
If you use a direct and an indirect object pronoun, the indirect one comes first. If they both begin with *l*, the indirect one changes to *se*.

e.g. *Ofrece los caramelos a Oscar* (She offers the sweets to Oscar) becomes *Se los ofrece* (She offers **them to him**).

When there are two verbs in the sentence and the second one is in the infinitive, the object pronouns can either go before the first verb, or at the end of the infinitive as part of the same word:
e.g. *Tenemos que mostrar la maleta a tus padres* (We have to show the briefcase to your parents) becomes *Se la tenemos que mostrar*, or *Tenemos que mostrársela* (We have to show **it** to **them**).

¿Has visto a Carlos?
Have you seen Carlos?

¿Sabes bailar salsa?
¿Do you know how to dance salsa?

¡Sí, está sonriéndome!
Yes, he's smiling at me!

Imperatives

With a verb in the imperative, any object pronoun goes on the end of the verb as part of the same word:
e.g. *¡Dámela!*
(Give it to me!)

With *no* and an imperative verb, though, you put the pronoun(s) between *no* and the verb:
e.g. *¡No **me la** des!*
(Don't show it to me!)

Quiero mandarlo hoy.
I want to send it today.

Dámelo.
Give it to me.

¡Cuidado!

Spanish does not use a word for "it" as a subject. It uses the verb alone. For "it" as a direct object, you use *lo* to refer to a masculine noun and *la* for a feminine noun. Referring to *el jersey* (sweater), for example, you would say *lo tengo* (I've got it), but referring to *la carta* (letter) you would say *la tengo* (I've got it). The indirect object "it" is always *le*.

Sí, voy a enseñarte.
Yes, I'm going to teach you.

53

The Salchicha treasure: chapter 12

Fede, Carmen and María realize that, in order to continue the hunt, they must first find the bald man. Perhaps his briefcase might be of some help...

Una agenda,
un periódico...

¡Mirad! Debajo hay
pedazos de papel.

Es una postal en
trozos pequeños.

Pero, ¿la
podemos leer?

Vocabulary

la agenda	diary
la comida	food, lunch
la dirección	address
la granja	farm
la linterna	(pocket) torch, flashlight
el pedazo/ el trozo	bit/piece
el roble	oak
la policía	the police
acercarse	to come next to (me/you...)
contar (ue)	to tell, to count
enseñar	to show, to teach
pasar	to pass, to hand
recomendar (ie)	to recommend
apasionante	exciting
buen viaje	(have a) good journey/trip
preparado/a	prepared/ready
tienda de campaña	tent
de todas formas	anyhow

The torn postcard provides vital information for Fede, Carmen and María, once they have worked out how the pieces join together.

muy apasionante.
una habitación
La casa es
buena. Bue

Querido Ramón
Gracias por tu carta
Campos viven cerca
pides su dirección

de los tres Robles, Carre
Nuevo, cerca de Pue
por qué Villatorres?

Ramón Robón
Calle Palencia 59
28040 Madrid

Sí, Antonia y Ana
de Villatorres. me
Aquí esta: La Granja

de todas formas, tienen
por ti y yo te los recomiendo.
tranquila, y la comida es
no, buen viaje.
Isabel

tera del Puente
rto Viejo. Pero
No es un pueblo

Try writing out the postcard with all the pieces in the right order. Can you figure out what it says?

Using the imperfect tense

There are several tenses you can use to describe actions in the past. One of them is called the imperfect. In Spanish, you use the imperfect to describe events that were in the process of happening, or things that used to happen often. For example: *Tocaba en un grupo* (He used to play in a band) or *Todos los sábados jugaba al fútbol* (Every Saturday he played soccer).

Making the imperfect

You make the imperfect of a verb by adding a special set of endings to its stem. There are two sets of endings: one for verbs ending in *-ar*, and one for verbs ending in *-er* or *-ir* (see right). Three common Spanish verbs, *ir, ver* and *ser,* have irregular imperfect forms. They are all shown here.

Ir (imperfect tense)

yo iba	I was going/ went (often)
tú ibas	you were going
él/ella iba	he/she/it was going
nosotros íbamos	we were going
vosotros ibais	you were going
ellos iban	they were going

Imperfect endings

For *-ar* verbs: *yo (-aba), tú (-abas), él/ella (-aba), nosotros (-abamos), vosotros (-abais),* and *ellos (-aban).* For *-er* and *-ir* verbs: *yo (-ía), tú (ías), él/ella (-ía), nosotros (-íamos), vosotros (-íais),* and *ellos (-ían).*

Ver (imperfect tense)

yo veía	I saw
tú veías	you saw
él/ella veía	he/she/it saw
nosotros veíamos	we saw
vosotros veíais	you saw
ellos veían	they saw

Ser (imperfect tense)

yo era	I was
tú eras	you were
él/ella era	he/she/it was
nosotros éramos	we were
vosotros erais	you were
ellos eran	they were

¿Dónde ibas anoche a las nueve?
Where were you going last night at nine o'clock?

Uh... iba a la casa de un amigo.
Umm... I was going to a friend's house.

Fast facts

The most useful verbs to learn in the imperfect are *tener, ir, ser* and *estar.* They are often used in this tense.

Translating the imperfect

There are many different ways to translate the Spanish imperfect tense into English:

• For actions that were in the process of happening, you can use "was" or "were" + a verb ending in "-ing", e.g. *gritaba* (I was shouting).

• For repeated or habitual actions in the past, you often use "used to" or "would" + an infinitive, e.g. *Tocaba la trompeta todos los días.* (I used to play the trumpet every day.)

• In English, you can often use the simple past tense ("I lived", "she went", etc.) to describe a repeated or continuous action in the past: e.g. *Todos los veranos, Pablo trabajaba en una cafetería.* (Every summer, Pablo worked in a café.)

Describing things

The imperfect tense is often used when giving descriptions of people: e.g. *El hombre **era** alto y calvo.* (The man was tall and bald.)

Here are some useful descriptive words in Spanish:

alto/a	tall
antipático/a	disagreeable/ unpleasant
bajo/a	short
delgado/a	thin
feo/a	ugly
gordo/a	fat
guapo/a	handsome/ beautiful
simpático/a	nice
la boca	mouth
el brazo	arm
la nariz	nose
el ojo	eye
el pelo	hair
la pierna	leg

Cuando Alfonso era joven... (When Alfonso was young...)

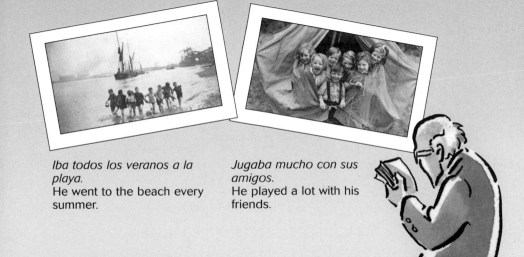

Iba todos los veranos a la playa.
He went to the beach every summer.

Jugaba mucho con sus amigos.
He played a lot with his friends.

The Salchicha treasure: chapter 13

The next morning, they take the briefcase to the police, along with the photo of the bald man which María took at the harbour. But they don't get the response they were expecting...

Entonces, ¿dónde estaba este maletín?

Estaba encima de la fotocopiadora del colegio.

¿Y por qué estabais vosotros allí?

Porque estamos buscando un tesoro...

...y había una pista en el colegio.

¿Qué tesoro?

Es de mi familia.

Ah, ya entiendo, y este estafador lo quiere robar...

¡Exactamente! La pista es una foto antigua.

Ayer por la noche la foto ya no estaba allí...

...pero encontramos el maletín del estafador.

Probablemente es el maletín de un profesor.

No, el estafador lo tenía antes.

¡Ya basta! Regresad a casa.

After the trio have left the office...

Devuelve este maletín al colegio ahora mismo.

¡Qué le vamos a hacer! Tendremos que seguir sin la policía.

Vocabulary

el bolsillo	pocket
el estafador	crook, swindler
la familia	family
el profesor	teacher
devolver (ue)	to bring/take back
regresar	to come/go (back)
robar	to steal, to rob
seguir (i)	to carry on, to continue
afortunadamente	fortunately
antes	before
ayer por la noche	yesterday evening
bonito/a	pretty
entonces	so
exactamente	exactly
había	there was/were
probablemente	probably
¡Qué le vamos a hacer!	what can we do! (too bad!)
sin	without
todavía	still

Afortunadamente sabemos la dirección del hombre calvo.

¡Eh, mirad! Todavía tengo la agenda que estaba en el maletín.

Estaba en mi bolsillo.

Using adverbs

Adverbs are words like "slowly" or "nicely" that give extra meaning to a verb. There are three main types:
- adverbs of **time** indicate **when** the action happens;
- adverbs of **place** describe **where** the action happens;
- adverbs of **manner** specify **how** the action happens.

How the action happens

Most Spanish adverbs of manner are just adjectives in their feminine form, with -*mente* on the end:
e.g. *rápida* + *mente* = *rapidamente*
(quick + ly = quickly)

If two or more adverbs of manner come together, -*mente* is only placed after the last one. The others take the feminine singular form of the adjective:
e.g. *Trabajo rápida y eficientemente.*
(I work quickly and efficiently.)

Prefiero ir más rauda y elegantemente.
I prefer to go more quickly and stylishly.

Irregular adverbs

Adjective	Adverb
bueno	*bien*
(good)	(well)
malo	*mal*
(bad)	(badly)
mucho	*mucho, muy*
(a lot of)	(a lot, very)
poco	*poco*
(little, few)	(little)

Useful adverbs

Time

a menudo	often
anoche	last night
a veces	sometimes
ayer	yesterday
ayer por la tarde	yesterday evening
antes de ayer	the day before yesterday
entonces	then
hoy	today
mañana	tomorrow
normalmente	usually, normally
nunca	never
pasado mañana	the day after tomorrow
siempre	always
todavía	still, yet
ya	already

Place

aquí	here
(por) allí	(over) there
lejos (de)	far (from)
por aquí	over/around here
en todas partes	everywhere
cerca (de)	near (to)
en alguna parte	somewhere
en ninguna parte	nowhere

Manner

afortunadamente	luckily
casi	almost, nearly
exactamente	exactly
lentamente	slowly
probablemente	probably
quizá(s)	maybe
rápidamente	quickly
realmente	really

Using two adverbs

In the sentence "the boy runs very quickly", "very" and "quickly" are both adverbs. "Very" describes how quickly the boy runs. This is called modifying the adverb.

Here is a list of Spanish adverbs that can modify other adverbs or adjectives:

menos	less
más	more
muy	very
demasiado	too much

e.g. *¡Anda muy rápidamente!*
(He's walking very fast!)

Expressions with *más*

Más is used in lots of different expressions. Here are some of them:

Más o menos	More or less
Por más que...	No matter how hard...
¡Es más (tonto/a)!	He's/She's so (silly)!

Word order

Some adverbs of time or place, such as *aquí* and *cerca*, can either come at the beginning or the end of a phrase. For instance, you can either say *Aquí hablamos español* or *Hablamos español aquí*. (We speak Spanish here.)

In general, most adverbs go after the first verb in a phrase:
e.g. *Llueve demasiado en Inglaterra.*
(It rains too much in England.)

e gusta mucho cantar.
e likes singing a lot.

Toca bien la guitarra.
He plays the guitar well

Toca demasiado rápidamente.
She plays too quickly.

Toca mal.
He plays badly.

After leaving the police station, Fede finds a note and an interesting magazine cutting in the bald man's diary. It seems that he has recently been involved in illegal activities...

Pájaros en extinción en las islas Lorazul

Hace cien años, había muchos loros azules en las islas Lorazul. Los habitantes los adoraban y construían templos para ellos. Estos pájaros ahora están en extinción y está prohibido capturarlos. El año pasado, se podía ver alguno de vez en cuando en Kuku, una isla desierta remota.

Señor Robón:

Encuéntreme una pareja de loros azules para mi colección. Su remuneración: 15.000 euros.

Señora Buitre

¡Eh! Las islas Lorazul... mi bisabuelo iba a menudo allí para estudiar las plantas.

Era botánico...

Y el hombre calvo estaba en esas islas para robar loros.

Venid, os quiero enseñar una cosa en casa.

Back at home, María shows Fede and Carmen a very old letter written to her grandfather, Santiago. It's from the governor of the Lorazul islands. It tells how her great-grandfather, Sancho, disappeared on one of the islands.

Villaloros

Señor

Por desgracia, probablemente su padre esté muerto. Conocía bien nuestras islas, pero en el momento de su desaparición buscaba plantas en unas islas peligrosas y muy remotas. Estaba con dos amigos botánicos. Llevaban un buen barco, pero era la temporada de lluvias.

Pedro Peperoni
Gobernador de las islas

Vocabulary

el año	year
bisabuelo/a	great-grandfather/ grandmother
el/la botánico/a	botanist
cien	one hundred
la colección	collection
la desaparición	disappearance
el gobernador	governor
el habitante	inhabitant
el loro	parrot
la pareja	couple, pair
la planta	plant
la remuneración	payment, fee
el templo	temple
la temporada de lluvias	stormy season
adorar	to worship
capturar	to catch
construir*	to build
estudiar	to study
parecer	to look/appear
interesante	interesting
pasado/a	last, past
peligroso/a	dangerous
prohibido/a	it is forbidden to
remoto/a	remote, faraway
cosa	thing
de vez en cuando	from time to time
en el momento de	at the time of
muerto/a	dead
por desgracia	unfortunately/ sadly

The preterite tense

The preterite tense is the most common past tense in Spanish. It is used to talk about once-only events that happened in the past, as opposed to events that were happening, or used to happen regularly. For example: *Compré pan.* (I bought bread.)

How to form the preterite

To form the preterite, you usually take the stem of the verb and add a special set of endings. There is one set of endings for *-ar* verbs, and another set for *-er* and *-ir* verbs.

pronoun	*ar* verbs	*er/ir* verbs
yo	-é	-í
tú	-aste	-iste
él/ella	-ó	-ió
nosotros	-amos	-imos
vosotros	-asteis	-isteis
ellos	-aron	-ieron

e.g. *Caminaron hacia la playa.*
(They walked to the beach.)
Comió a las seis.
(He ate at six.)
En 1998, viví en Madrid.
(In 1998, I lived in Madrid.)

¡Ayer encontré mis llaves!
(Yesterday I found my keys!)

¿Qué hiciste ayer por la tarde?
What did you do yesterday evening?

Leí un libro y ví la tele.
I read a book and watched TV.

Useful vocabulary

Sentences in the preterite tense often use a set of words and phrases called temporal complements. These describe a time in the past which has ended. Here are some useful examples:

ayer	yesterday
la semana pasada	last week
el año pasado	last year
hace un mes	one month ago
a principios de(l) (siglo)	at the beginning of (the century)
en el pasado	in the past
en 1940	in 1940
hace tiempo	a while ago
antes de...	before...

Other irregular verbs

Some Spanish verbs ending in -car, -gar, -zar have an irregular preterite, for the *yo* form of the verb. All the other endings are regular:

For verbs ending in -car, e.g. *buscar* (to look for), the *c* changes to **qu**: e.g. *Busqué mis llaves.* (I looked for my keys.)

For verbs ending in -gar, e.g. *llegar* (to arrive), the *g* changes to **gu**: e.g. *Llegué tarde.* (I arrived late.)

For verbs ending in -zar, e.g. *empezar* (to start), the *z* changes to a *c*: e.g. *Empecé a leer.* (I started to read.)

Preterite or imperfect?

Often you will find both the imperfect and the preterite tense in one sentence. The imperfect tense is used to set the scene, describe how things were, and talk about continuous actions. The preterite tense is used for actions which only happened once, and interrupted or altered the situation:

e.g. *Estaba leyendo cuando el teléfono sonó.* (I was reading when the phone rang.)

Fast facts

• If you're describing a one-off event that is over and done with, use the preterite tense.

• If you're setting the scene in the past, or talking of something that was in the process of happening, use the imperfect tense.

¿Tienes una moto nueva?
Have you got a new motorcycle?

La vi ayer.
¡Es superguai!
I saw it yesterday.
It's great!

La compré el sábado.
I bought it on Saturday.

65

The Salchicha treasure: chapter 15

While they're waiting for lunch, the three friends read in the bald man's diary how he came across details of the Salchicha treasure...

Logró llegar a la isla Kuku...

...A la entrada de una cueva, vio un cofre viejo.

Dentro encontró una carta que hablaba de un tesoro.

Sí, la carta que robó...

¡Venid a comer!, papá está aquí.

Lo siento, pero la reunión fue muy larga.

Vocabulary

el cofre	chest (container)
la cueva	cave
la entrada	entrance
la isla	island
el pan	bread
la reunión	meeting
la tienda (de campaña)	tent
comprar	to buy
dejar	to leave behind
esperar (a)	to wait, to hope for, to expect
hablar	to talk, speak
ir de compras	to go shopping
llegar	to reach, to arrive, to get to
llover (ue)	to rain
lograr	to manage
meter	to put in/inside
olvidarse	to forget
preocuparse	to worry
robar	to steal
terminar	to end, finish
venir	to come
cómo	how
como	as, like
dentro	inside
largo/a	long
lo siento	I'm sorry
no importa	it doesn't matter
papá	Dad, Daddy
viejo/a	old

More about preterites

Most verbs which are irregular in the present tense are also irregular in the preterite tense. Nearly all irregular preterite verbs follow a pattern which you can learn.

Irregular preterite endings

Most verbs with an irregular preterite have a special, preterite stem that you have to learn. Add the following endings to the stem:

pronoun	preterite ending
yo	-e
tú	-iste
él/ella	-o
nosotros	-imos
vosotros	-isteis
ellos	-ieron

Some useful irregular verbs and their preterite stems:

Infinitive	Preterite stem
andar (to walk)	anduv-
estar (to be)	estuv-
poner (to put)	pus-
querer (to want)	quis-
saber (to know)	sup-
tener (to have)	tuv-
venir (to come)	vin-
decir (to say)	dij-
traer (to bring)	traj-

Useful verbs

Here are some commonly used irregular preterite verbs with their endings. As you can see, they all follow the pattern described on the left:

Hacer (to do/make): *yo hice, tú hiciste, él/ella hizo, nosotros hicimos, vosotros hicisteis, ellos hicieron.*

Dar (to give) *yo di, tú diste, él/ella dio, nosotros dimos, vosotros disteis, ellos dieron.*

Ver (to see) *yo vi, tú viste, él/ella vio, nosotros vimos, vosotros visteis, ellos vieron.*

Ser (to be) and **ir** (to go) share the same preterite: *yo fui, tú fuiste, él/ella fue, nosotros fuimos, vosotros fuisteis, ellos fueron.*

 ¡Cuidado!

Three verbs are irregular in the present tense, but not in the preterite. They are: *conocer* (to know), *salir* (to go out), and *ver* (to see).

¡Estuve en Granada y Sevilla!
I was in Granada and Seville!

Which past tense?

The preterite tense describes things which happened in the past, and have ended. To describe a past action or ongoing period of time, use the present perfect tense: e.g. *Hoy he ido al colegio.* (Today I've been to school.) For more information about the present perfect tense, see page 72.

Fast facts

The preterite tense is always used to describe finished actions. Think about the period of time or the action you want to describe. If it has ended completely, you will need to use the preterite tense.

Stem-changing preterites

In the preterite, *-ar* stem-changing verbs and most *-er* stem-changing verbs have no stem change. They behave just like regular *-ar* and *-er* verbs (see page 64). *Poder* and *querer* are exceptions, as they have irregular preterites (see opposite page).

-Ir stem-changing verbs do have a stem change in the preterite. This only affects the *él/ella* and *ellos* forms, and involves an *e* changing to an *i*. These verbs take the same preterite endings as regular *-ir* verbs (see page 64):

e.g. *Pedí huevos fritos.*
(I ordered fried eggs.)
Pidío huevos fritos.
(He/She ordered fried eggs.)

Javier se levantó tarde esta mañana.
Javier woke up late this morning.

Se vistió rápidamente y fue corriendo a la escuela...
He dressed quickly and hurried to school...

...pero aún así llegó tarde.
...but he was still late.

Y desgraciadamente es el profesor!
And unfortunately, he's the teacher!

The Salchicha treasure: chapter 16

After lunch, Fede, Carmen and María go to the farm where the crook, Ramón Robón, is staying. When they arrive, they overhear a conversation that will take them to the next clue...

> *Tenemos que ir a la Granja de las Tres Robles...*

> *...para encontrar al señor Robón y la pista del colegio.*

> *¿Café, señor Robón?*

> *Gracias... em, quería hacerles una pregunta...*

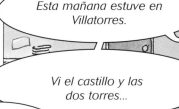

> *Esta mañana estuve en Villatorres.*

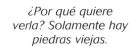

> *Vi el castillo y las dos torres...*

> *...pero no pude encontrar la torre en ruinas.*

> *¿Por qué quiere verla? Solamente hay piedras viejas.*

> *er... Me gustan las ruinas.*

Vale, ¿fue al parque?

Sí, pero no vi nada.

¡Ah! Usted no bajó hasta el rio...

Ah Antonia, ya estás despierta.

...sí, la torre en ruinas está al lado del río.

¿Ah, sí? Muy interesante...

La próxima pista debe estar en la torre vieja.

Vocabulary

el parque	park
la piedra	stone
la ruina	ruin
bajar	to go down
hacer una pregunta	to ask a question
al lado de	by (the side of)
algun**os/as**	a few
precios**o/a**	lovely/beautiful
en ruinas	ruined, in ruins
solamente	only

The perfect tense

The English perfect tense is made from "to have" and a form of the verb called the past participle, e.g. "I have eaten". Spanish also has a perfect tense that it uses in the same way, and in similar situations. It is made using the present tense of *haber* (a special verb for "to have").

Forms of *haber*

Haber is an irregular verb:
yo he
tú has
él/ella ha
nosotros hemos
vosotros habéis
ellos han

The past participle

Making the past participle of a verb is usually easy in Spanish. You just add *-ado* to the stem of *-ar* verbs, and *-ido* to the stem of *-er* and *-ir* verbs. The past participle comes after the appropriate form of the verb *haber*.
e.g. *He hablado con ella.*
I have spoken to her.
Some verbs are irregular, e.g. *escribir* (to write, past participle *escrito*).

Esta noche...
This evening...

He *llamado a mi hermana.*
I have phoned my sister.

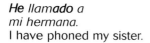

He *escrito una carta.*
I have written a letter.

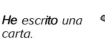

He *comido la cena.*
I have eaten dinner.

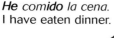

Fast facts

The phrase "have just" in English can be translated into Spanish without using the past participle. You use the verb *acabar de* (literally, "to finish"), and the infinitive of the other verb:
e.g. *Acabo de llegar.*
(I have just arrived.)
Mi jefe acaba de llamarme.
(My boss has just phoned me.)

Irregular past participles

Some verbs have irregular past participles. Here are some of the most useful ones:

Verb	Past participle
abrir (to open)	*abierto*
decir (to say)	*dicho*
devolver (to give back)	*devuelto*
escribir (to write)	*escrito*
freír (to fry)	*frito*
hacer (to do)	*hecho*
poner (to put)	*puesto*
ver (to see)	*visto*
volver (to go back)	*vuelto*

Mine, yours, his, etc.

For "mine", "yours", etc. Spanish has a special set of words (see right). These change to match the noun they are replacing, according to whether the noun is masculine or feminine, singular or plural.
So, talking about a bag (*un bolso*) you would say:
***El mío** es negro.*
(Mine is black.)
Talking about a suitcase (*una maleta*) you would say:
***La mía** es negra.*
(Mine is black.)

With the verb *ser*, you usually drop the words *el, la, los* and *las*: *Es mío/mía* (It's mine). Also, with *ser*, to say that something is "his", "hers" and "yours", you can either use *suyo* or *de + él/ella*. For example, you can say *El coche es **suyo**,* or *El coche es **de él*** (It's his).

Possessive pronouns

Singular

[m]	[f]	
el mío	la mía	mine
el tuyo	la tuya	yours
el suyo	la suya	hers/ his/its
el nuestro	la nuestra	ours
el vuestro	la vuestra	yours
el suyo	la suya	theirs

Plural

[m]	[f]	
los míos	las mías	mine
los tuyos	las tuyas	yours
los suyos	las suyas	hers/ his/its
los nuestros	las nuestras	ours
los vuestros	la vuestra	yours
los suyos	las suyas	theirs

¿De quién es? (Whose is it?)

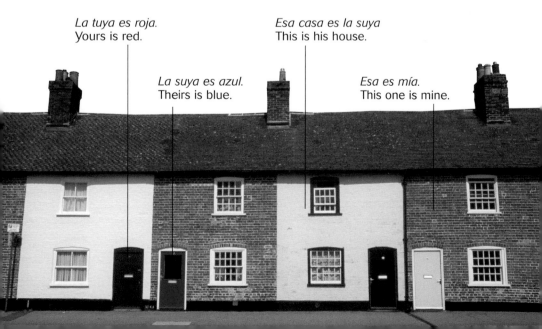

La tuya es roja.
Yours is red.

Esa casa es la suya
This is his house.

La suya es azul.
Theirs is blue.

Esa es mía.
This one is mine.

The Salchicha treasure: chapter 17

Fede, Carmen and María go home to get their bikes and rush to the ruined tower to find the next clue before Ramón gets there. It takes them quite a while to find it...

Soon they are at the tower ruins.

> ¡Nada!
> He buscado por todas partes y he examinado cada piedra.

> ¡Eh! he encontrado algo aquí.

> ¡Mirad... es la señal de Sancho Salchicha!

The three friends have found Sancho Salchicha's sign on an old plaque.

Hemos conservado esta torre en ruinas porque es un monumento sagrado para los habitantes de Villatorres.
Los piratas de la Isla de los Piratas la destruyeron hace tres años, pero ahora nosotros nos hemos vengado. Hemos ganado nuestra última batalla contra ellos, los hemos expulsado de su fuerte en la isla y han desaparecido de nuestro país.

Vocabulary

la bici	bike
la batalla	battle
el fuerte	fort
el monumento	monument
el país	country
el pirata	pirate
la valla	fence
conservar	to keep/ preserve
desaparecer	to disappear
descifrar	to decipher/to work out
destruir	to destroy
examinar	to examine
explorar	to explore
expulsar	to throw out/expel
ganar	to win/earn
necesitar	to need
vengarse	to get revenge
algo	something
cada	each
sagrado/a	sacred
todavía	yet, still
último/a	last

The words on the plaque give them a good idea of where they must go next. Translate it and see what you think...

The future tense

In Spanish, there are several ways of expressing the future:
- You can use the future tense (see below).
- You can use the verb *ir* (to go) with an infinitive, just as we do in English e.g. *voy a preparar la cena.* (I'm going to prepare supper.)
- You can indicate the future by using a word like *mañana* (tomorrow) with the present tense.

Making the future tense

The future endings are: *(yo)* -é, *(tu)* -ás, *(él/ella)* -á, *(nosotros)* -emos, *(vosotros)* -éis, *(ellos)* -án. In most cases, they are just added to the infinitive of the verb, but some verbs have irregular future stems (see right).

Andar (future)

yo andar**é**	I will walk
tú andar**ás**	you will walk
él/ella andar**á**	he/she/it will walk
nosotros andar**emos**	we will walk
vosotros andar**éis**	you will walk
ellos andar**án**	they will walk

Te daré el regalo esta noche, papá. I'll give you the present this evening, Dad.

Future vocabulary

mañana	tomorrow
la próxima semana	next week
el mes que viene	next month

Irregular future stems

There are some verbs that do not use the infinitive to form the future tense. Instead they have their own future stem. Here are some common irregular future stems:

decir (to say) - *dir-*
hacer (to do, to make) - *har-*
poder (to be able to, can) - *podr-*
poner (to put) - *pondr-*
querer (to want) - *querr-*
saber (to know) - *sabr-*
salir (to go out) - *saldr-*
tener (to have) - *tendr-*
venir (to come) - *vendr-*

Stem-changing verbs do not have a stem change in the future tense. You form the future in the same way as you do for regular verbs, using the infinitive of the verb and the future endings. The exceptions are *querer* and *poder* (see above).

Learning tip

Don't forget the accents when writing in the future tense. Every form of any verb, except for the *nosotros* form, has an accented vowel in the ending.

Using the present

Sometimes both Spanish and English use the present tense when talking about future events:
e.g. *Regreso hoy por la tarde.*
(I'm coming back this evening.)
The time words ("tomorrow", "this evening", etc.) already indicate that the action will happen in the future, so you don't need to use the future tense as well.

¡Salgo mañana por la mañana!
I'm leaving tomorrow morning!

Going to...

In both Spanish and English, you can also express the future by using the verb "to go", e.g. *Voy a abrir la puerta* (I'm going to open the door). This is fairly common in Spanish, especially when talking about events that are just about to happen. You take the present tense of *ir* (to go) and add an infinitive. So, "I'm going to make a cake" would be *Voy a hacer un pastel.*

Fast facts

The three ways of talking about future events are:

• infinitive or future stem + *é, ás, á, emos, éis, án*

• *ir* (present tense) + *a* + infinitive

• present tense of verb + time word indicating the future

Using *si*

In sentences starting with the word *si* (if), the second of the two verbs which follow is usually in the future tense:

e.g. *Si llueve me quedaré en casa.*
(If it rains, I'll stay at home.)

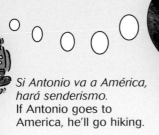

Si Antonio va a América, hará senderismo.
If Antonio goes to America, he'll go hiking.

The Salchicha treasure: chapter 18

Fede, Carmen and María need to go to the fort on Pirates' Island, but it's too late to go that night. Just in case Ramón finds the clue and gets ahead of them, they devise a very crafty way of throwing him off the scent...

*Fede y yo podemos buscar
un buen sitio.*

A few minutes later...

*Podemos esconder
la nota aquí y dibujar
su señal.*

*¡Qué buena idea!
Seguro que caerá en
la trampa.*

María writes a note to confuse the
crook and put him on a false trail.

*.S.S sóidA. illa nátse anutrof im y sayoj
sim sadoT. aredam ed selenap noc derap
anu sárartnocne ortneD. illa rop
sárartnE. setorrab nis anatnev anu
sáreV. ojeiV otreuP ed airasimoc al a ri
euq sárdneT. licífid éreS. nóisim amitlú
ut átse iuqA. odajed eh euq satsip sal
sadot odartnocne sah arohA
:ojih odireuQ.*

Vocabulary

el barrote	(window) bar
la fortuna	fortune
la hoja	leaf, sheet (of paper)
la joya	jewel
la madera	wood
la misión	task
el panel	panel
la señal	sign
el sitio	place
la tierra	earth, ground
la trampa	trap
caer en la trampa	to fall in the trap
dibujar	to draw
dejar	to leave (behind)
molestar	to disturb
dentro	inside
durante	during
falso/a	false
por allí	over there
seguro que	definitely, most probably

Can you read María's writing and find out where she is sending
Ramón the crook?

The Salchicha treasure: chapter 19

That evening, the policeman who didn't believe the three friends' story stumbles across Ramón Robón's picture in the wanted files. Then he lands a catch he hadn't been anticipating...

Meanwhile, outside the police station…

Primero, voy a cenar y volveré después. Será muy de noche.

Sometime later…

Ah, por fin…

Vocabulary

el/la chico/a	boy/girl
el detalle	detail
el número	number
la recompensa	reward
el robo	theft
la ventana	window
ayudar	to help
cenar	to have supper
quedar	to be/remain
romper	to break
¡alto!	stop!
después	later/then
detenido/a	under arrest
por fin	at last
41 años	41 years old

Número 7454
Ramón Robón
41 años

Se busca por robo
Recompensa

Bien, mañana iré a la casa Salchicha.

Probablemente los chicos podrán ayudarme a encontrarlo.

Then suddenly…

¿Pero qué ha sido eso?

¡Es él! ¡Eh… Alto! Queda usted detenido.

Making comparisons

In English, you make comparisons either by adding "more" or "the most" before the descriptive word, or by adding "-er" or "-est" to the end of the word. Comparisons can be made with either adjectives or adverbs.

Comparisons with adjectives

In Spanish, to make comparisons with adjectives, you normally use the word *más* (to mean "-er" or "**more**") and **el/la/los/las más** (to mean "**the -est**" or "**the most**"). These go before the adjective. Remember that the adjective must always agree with the noun it's describing (see page 12).

el más alto
the tallest

la más baja
the shortest

más alto
taller

Bigger than, smaller than

In English, we link the two things we are comparing with "than" (e.g. Peter is bigger **than** Paul, the violin is smaller **than** the cello, etc.). In Spanish, the linking word is *que*:
e.g. *Es más alto que su hermana.*
(He is taller **than** his sister.)

To say something is "(just) **as... as**", for example "(just) as hard-working as", you use *tan... como*:
e.g. *Es tan trabajador como su hermana.*
He's **just as** hard-working **as** his sister.

Less, the least

To make comparisons such as "less interesting" and "the least difficult" you use *menos* (less) in the same way as *más* and *el menos* (the least) in the same way as *el más.*
e.g. *Este tema es menos interesante.*
(This subject is **less interesting**.)
El vestido menos caro.
(The **least expensive** dress.)

Comparisons with adverbs

You make comparisons with adverbs in Spanish in almost the same way as you do with adjectives. *Más* is used, but there is no agreement, because they are describing the action, not the noun.
e.g. *Anda más lentamente.*
(He walks **more slowly**.)

The "-est/the most" form with adverbs is very complicated in Spanish, and hardly ever used.

Fast facts

With the expressions *el/la/los/las más/menos*, you need to add the word *de* (of):
e.g. *Ana es la chica más simpática de la clase.*
(Ana is the nicest girl in the class.)

Some exceptions

Some Spanish comparative adjectives and adverbs are irregular:

Adjectives

bueno/a	*mejor*	*el/la/los/las mejor(-es)*
good	better	the best
malo/a	*peor*	*el/la/los/las peor(-es)*
bad	worse	the worst
grande	*mayor*	*el/la/los/las mayor(-es)*
big	bigger	the biggest
pequeño/a	*menor*	*el/le/los/las menor(-es)*
small	smaller	the smallest

Adverbs

bien	*mejor*
well	better
mal	*peor*
bad	worse

Older and younger

The word for "old" in Spanish is *viejo*, but in comparisons you use the word ***mayor*** ("bigger" in English), to mean "older" or "oldest":

e.g. *Pedro es **el mayor**.*
(Pedro is **the oldest**.)

Similarly, the Spanish word for young is *joven*, but you can use the word ***menor*** ("smaller" in English) to mean "younger" or "youngest":

e.g. *María es **menor que** Pedro.*
(Maria is **younger than** Pedro.)

Las velas más altas son también las más pequeñas.
The highest sails are also the smallest ones.

Este barco es mucho más grande que los otros.
This boat is much bigger than the others.

Ese barco está más cerca.
This boat is nearer.

Aquel está más lejos.
That one is further away.

83

The Salchicha treasure: chapter 20

The next morning, the three friends borrow Rafa's boat to cross to Pirates' Island. They get inside the ruined fort, but can they find the treasure and get out again?

¡Qué raro! La puerta suele estar cerrada.

¡Eh, id más despacio!

¡Oh, no!

Mirad, hay cuatro túneles.

¡No!

¡Ahora no podemos salir!

¡Venid aquí! ¡Mirad!

EL TÚNEL MÁS LARGO AL FINAL

The three friends must go to the end of the longest tunnel. They measure the tunnels using footsteps. Fede and María each take one and Carmen does the other two.

Mi túnel no es tan largo como el tuyo.

Mi primer túnel era tan largo como el tuyo, pero mi segundo túnel es más corto.

El mío es más largo que el primer túnel de Carmen.

Vocabulary

el calabozo	dungeon
el fuerte	fort
la puerta	door
el remo	oar
la toalla	towel
el túnel	tunnel
bajar	to come down/get off
prestar	to lend
remar	to row
soler	to be in the habit of/to usually
corto/a	short
al final de	at/to the end of
mojado/a	wet
otro/a	other, another
raro/a	weird, strange

Do you know which tunnel they must take?

85

Conditional sentences

A conditional action is one that depends on something else happening. In both Spanish and English you often use a special set of conditional verb endings to describe conditional actions, for example: *Jugaría al fútbol, pero hace demasiado calor.* (I would play football, but it's too hot.) Conditionals can also be used in polite expressions, for example: *¿Podrías abrir la ventana?* (Could you open the window?)

Making the conditional

Making the conditional is easy in Spanish for most verbs. You just take the stem of the future tense (which is usually the infinitive of the verb), and add the *-er* and *-ir* imperfect tense verb endings (*-ía, -ías, -ía, -íamos, -íais, -ían*).

> *Jugar* (conditional)
>
> | | |
> |---|---|
> | *yo jugaría* | I would play |
> | *tu jugarías* | you would play |
> | *él/ella jugaría* | he/she/it would play |
> | *nosotros jugaríamos* | we would play |
> | *vosotros jugaríais* | you would play |
> | *ellos jugarían* | they would play |

Compraría esta casa, pero no tengo dinero.
I would buy this house, but I don't have any money.

If

In Spanish, the word for "if" is *si*. Like "if", you can use it with various tenses depending on what you are saying.

You can use *si* with the present and future tenses, in the same way as you use "if" in English:
e.g. *Si el profesor sale de la clase, los niños juegan.*
(If the teacher leaves the classroom, the children play.)
Si tengo tiempo, voy contigo.
(If I have time, I'll come with you.)

For things you are imagining, use *si* with the verb that follows it in a tense called the imperfect subjunctive. The "would" verb of the sentence goes in the conditional. To form the imperfect subjunctive, you take the *ellos* form of the preterite (see page 62), drop *on* from the end and add the endings: *-a, -as, -a, -amos, -ais, -an.*
e.g. *Si tuviera mucho dinero, iría a Nueva York.*
(If I had lots of money, I'd go to New York.)

> ### Fast facts
>
> Conditional = stem of future tense + *-er* / *-ir* imperfect tense verb ending.

Irregular conditionals

Irregular conditional verbs all have regular conditional endings, but a different stem which you have to learn. Here are some useful ones:

Infinitive	Conditional stem
decir	*dir-*
haber	*habr-*
hacer	*har-*
poder	*podr-*
querer	*querr-*

Quisiera una tarta de chocolate y un helado de fresa y...
I'd like a chocolate cake and a strawberry ice cream and...

Fast facts

Use the conditional when talking about conditional actions, or asking for something politely.

Polite conversation

The conditional can be used in polite conversation. A polite way to ask someone to do something, for example, is to use the conditional and say *podría* (may/could):
e.g. *¿Podrías darme un vaso de agua?*
(Could you give me a glass of water?)

A more polite way of asking for something is to use the imperfect subjunctive, and say *quisiera* (which also translates as "I would like"):
e.g. *Quisiera un vaso de agua.*
(I would like a glass of water.)

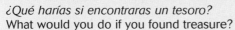

¿Qué harías si encontraras un tesoro?
What would you do if you found treasure?

Haría un crucero.
I would go on a cruise.

Iría a la luna.
I would go to the moon.

The Salchicha treasure: chapter 21

The three friends select the longest tunnel. Now, if there's any treasure to be found, surely they must be close...

Meanwhile, the policeman has gone to the Salchicha house...

¡Hola! Quisiera hablar con María, Carmen y Fede.

Vocabulary

la anilla	ring
el estafador	crook, swindler
el hierro	iron
la historia	history, story
la luz	light
atrapar	to catch
ayudar	to help
contar	to tell/recount
dar las gracias	to thank
encontrar	to meet
esperar	to wait
molestar	to disturb
querer	to want
saber	to know
terminar	to end, to finish
primero	first
si	if
tal vez	maybe

Me gustaría darles las gracias. Me ayudaron a atrapar a un estafador.

¿Querría esperarles?

No, ya volveré, no quisiera molestarles.

Pero primero, tal vez usted podría contarnos la historia. No sabemos nada.

Writing a letter in Spanish

There are two main types of letter: informal (for friends and family) and formal (for companies and people you don't know). Here are some basic guidelines for writing letters in Spanish.

Structure

Every letter has a basic structure. Normally, you put your town or full address in the top right-hand corner, followed by the date. At the end, you sign off with an appropriate farewell.

The date

If the date is Tuesday 7th September, you can either write *martes, 7 de septiembre* (Tuesday, 7 of September) or just *7 de septiembre* (7 of September). Days of the week and month are listed on page 94. Remember that, unlike English, the words for months and days of the week don't have a capital letter.

Madrid, 8 de octubre

Querida María,

Gracias por tu carta. ¿Cómo estás? Yo estoy muy bien. Me han tocado dos entradas para un concierto en noviembre. ¿Quieres acompañarme? ¡Nos lo pasaremos muy bien!

Escríbeme pronto

Muchos besos de
Antonia

Informal letters

The Spanish for "dear" is *querido*. You use it when writing to friends and family and people you know very well. Because *querido* is an adjective, you have to make it agree with the noun which follows.
• Before a male name you write *querido,* e.g. *Querido Juan.*
• Before a female name you write *querida,* e.g. *Querida María.*
• Before more than one male name or a mixture of male and female names you use *queridos*: e.g. *Queridos Juan y María.*
• Before more than one female name you use *queridas*: e.g. *Queridas María y Susana.*

Useful phrases

• *Gracias por...* (Thanks for...) e.g. *Gracias por tu carta.* (Thanks for your letter.)
• *Me alegré mucho al recibir tu carta.* (It was very good to get your letter).
• *Siento no haberte escrito antes, pero he estado muy ocupado/a.* I'm sorry I haven't written for so long, but I've been very busy.

Signing off

Use *Con cariño* (best wishes) for people you know quite well. For close friends and family, you can use *Abrazos/Besos de* (hugs/kisses from), or *Muchos besos de* (lots of kisses from).

Signing off

The usual way to finish a letter to a firm or someone you don't know is *Atentamente*.

The equivalent in English is "Yours faithfully".

Formal letters

If you're writing to someone that you've never met before, you use *estimado/a*, or *estimados/as* for a group of people, followed by the appropriate address. Like *querido*, *estimado* is an adjective, so it changes in the same way (see previous page):
• *Estimados señores* (Dear sirs)
• *Estimado señor* (Dear sir)
• *Estimada señora* (Dear madam)
If you know the person's surname, put it after the title
(e.g. *señor Salchicha*).

Useful phrases

• *Me gustaría recibir información sobre...* (Please give me details of...)
• *Escribo para preguntar si...* (I am writing to ask whether...)
• *Podría enviarme...* (Please send me...)
• *Adjunto...* (I enclose...)
• *Me gustaría reservar...* (I would like to reserve...)
• *Gracias de antemano* (Thank you in advance for...)
• *En espera de sus noticias...* (I look forward to hearing from you...)
• *Se despide atentamente...* (Yours sincerely...)

> 59 Kipling Street
> London SE1 3RZ
>
> 29. de julio
>
> Oficina de turismo,
> C/de la Paz no. 8,
> Andorra 34607
>
> Estimado señor,
>
> Este verano voy de vacaciones a los Pirineos con mi famila y me gustaría saber algo más de la región. ¿Podría enviarme folletos acerca de esa área? Estaría especialmente interesado en información sobre zonas de acampada.
>
> Atentamente,
> Paul Smith

How do I make the conditional of the verb *gustar*?

91

The Salchicha treasure: chapter 22

Back at the old fort, they've found the treasure, and now just have to find a way out since the entrance has been jammed by fallen rocks...

¡Rápido! Tenemos que buscar una salida.

¡Mirad! ¡Luz!

Seguramente encontraremos una, si volvemos a los escalones.

¡Uf!

Carmen, si mueves esas piedras, nadie podrá ver la entrada.

Vocabulary

el/la adolescente	teenager
el escalón	step
el estafador	thief
el héroe	hero
la muerte	death
Navidad	Christmas
el oro	gold
la recompensa	reward
el reproductor de CDs	CD player
abandonado/a	abandoned, left
dirigido/a a	addressed to
encontrarse (ue)	to find by chance/ to come across
estar de acuerdo	to agree
felicitar	to congratulate
lanzar	to launch
lograr	to achieve/attain
mover	to move
pasar	to pass, to spend time
parar	to stop, end up
perder	to lose
recibir	to receive
durante	during
hasta pronto	see you soon

¡Le podré regalar a Rafa un par de remos nuevos!

And so the three friends make it home to a hero's welcome.

Once Fede and Carmen are back home in Madrid, María sends them a letter and a cutting from the local newspaper...

Villatorres, lunes 2 de septiembre

Queridos Fede y Carmen:

Aquí está el artículo de "La Voz de Villatorres" que cuenta nuestra historia. ¡Es fenomenal! ¿Qué vais a hacer con vuestra parte de la recompensa? Con la mía, voy a comprar un reproductor de CDs.
Si vuestra madre está de acuerdo, iré a vuestra casa durante las vacaciones de Navidad, así que ¡hasta pronto!, espero.

Muchos besos de

María

LA VOZ DE VILLATORRES

——— Viernes, 30 de agosto ———

El tesoro de la familia Salchicha

María Salchicha con sus amigos Fede y Carmen y su perro Guau Guau.

Ramón Robón, el ladrón de pájaros en extinción que quería robar el tesoro de la familia Salchicha.

María Salchicha y sus amigos Fede y Carmen han pasado un mes de agosto apasionante: encontraron un tesoro y ayudaron a la policía a atrapar a un estafador, Ramón Robón.

Hace unos meses Robón fue a las islas Lorazul porque quería robar loros en extinción. Allí encontró en un cofre viejo una carta que el bisabuelo de María, Sancho, había escrito a su hijo Santiago. Robón leyó la carta y se lanzó a la búsqueda del tesoro. Así llegó a Villatorres, donde perdió la carta. Esta fue a parar a manos de Fede y Carmen, que habían venido a pasar unos días con su amiga María.

Los tres adolescentes siguieron las pistas que daba la carta. Así lograron encontrar el tesoro que estaba escondido en el viejo Fuerte de los Piratas antes que el estafador y ayudaron a la policía a atraparlo.

La policía ha entregado a los tres jóvenes 2.000 euros de recompensa. Desde "La Voz de Villatorres" felicitamos a los tres héroes.

93

Numbers and other useful words

Los números (numbers)

0	cero	18	dieciocho
1	uno	19	diecinueve
2	dos	20	veinte
3	tres	21	veintiuno
4	cuatro	22	veintidós
5	cinco	23	veintitrés
6	seis	30	treinta
7	siete	31	treinta y uno
8	ocho	40	cuarenta
9	nueve	50	cincuenta
10	diez	60	sesenta
11	once	70	setenta
12	doce	71	setenta y uno
13	trece	72	setenta y dos
14	catorce	80	ochenta
15	quince	81	ochenta y uno
16	dieciséis	90	noventa
17	diecisiete	91	noventa y uno

100	cien
101	ciento uno
150	ciento cincuenta
200	doscientos
201	doscientos uno
300	trescientos

1,000	mil
1,100	mil cien
1,200	mil doscientos
2,000	dos mil
2,100	dos mil cien
10,000	diez mil
100,000	cien mil
1,000,000	un millón

1st	1º/1ª	(el/la) primero(a)
2nd	2º	(el/la) segundo(a)
3rd	3º	(el/la) tercero(a)
9th	9º	(el/la) noveno(a)

When accompanying or replacing feminine nouns, *uno* changes into *una*. For all numbers over 99 accompanying feminine nouns, *-cientos* changes into *-cientas*.

Los días (days)

lunes [m]	Monday
martes [m]	Tuesday
miércoles [m]	Wednesday
jueves [m]	Thursday
viernes [m]	Friday
sábado [m]	Saturday
domingo [m]	Sunday

Los meses (months)

enero	January
febrero	February
marzo	March
abril	April
mayo	May
junio	June
julio	July
agosto	August
septiembre	September
octubre	October
noviembre	November
diciembre	December

Las fechas (dates)

¿Qué día es hoy?	What's the date today?
el lunes	on Monday
todos los lunes	every Monday
en agosto/ en el mes de agosto	in August
el uno de abril	April the first
martes, 7 de septiembre	Tuesday September 7th

Los años (years)

1980	mil novecientos ochenta
2000	dos mil
2001	dos mil uno
2002	dos mil dos
2010	dos mil diez

Las estaciones (seasons)

la primavera	spring
el verano	summer
el otoño	autumn
el invierno	winter

El tiempo (weather)

el clima	climate
el prónostico del tiempo	weather forecast
la temperatura	temperature
¿Qué tiempo hace?	What's the weather like?
Hace buen tiempo	It's fine
Hace calor	It's hot
Hace sol	It's sunny
Hace frío	It's cold
Hace malo	It's bad
Nieva/está nevando	It's snowing
Llueve/Está lloviendo	It's raining
Hay niebla	It's foggy
Hay hielo	It's icy
El sol brilla	The sun's shining
el relámpago	lightning
la escarcha	frost
el hielo	ice
el granizo	hail
la nieve	snow
la nube	cloud
la tormenta	storm
la lluvia	rain
el sol	sun
el trueno	thunder

Useful words

hasta pronto	see you soon
hasta luego	see you later
adiós	goodbye
hola	hello
buenas noches	good night
buenas tardes	good evening, good afternoon
buenos días	good morning
de nada	you're welcome
gracias	thank you
no	no
si	yes
perdón	excuse me
quizá(s)	maybe
por favor	please
lo siento	I'm sorry

Useful expressions

¿Cómo se dice esto en español?
(How do you say this in Spanish?)
No comprendo.
(I don't understand.)
¿Puedes repetir, por favor?
Can you repeat that, please?
No sé.
(I don't know.)
Siento saber que...
(I'm sorry to hear that...)
¿Qué significa esto?
(What does this mean?)

¿Cómo se dice "it's hot" en español?

Se dice "hace calor".

Spain and Latin America

Spanish is one of the most widely spoken languages in the world. It is the official language of 20 countries, and spoken by more than 200 million people worldwide.

Languages in Spain

Spain has four official national languages. They are Castilian Spanish, Catalan, Galician and Basque. The first three of these languages are derived from Latin. The Spanish in this book is Castilian Spanish.

• **Castilian Spanish** is the most widely spoken language in Spain. It is also spoken throughout most of Central and South America. However, there are lots of different dialects of Castillian Spanish, and lots of different forms of pronounciation. In southern Spain for example, the letter *c* before *e* or *i* is not lisped, as it is in the rest of the country.

• **Catalan** is spoken in Catalonia, in the north-east of Spain, in coastal Valencia, and in the Balearic islands (Majorca, Menorca and Ibiza). In these areas it is the official language alongside Castilian Spanish, and is taught in schools.

• **Galician** is the third Latin-based language of Spain. It is a very different language to Castilian Spanish, sounding closer to Portuguese. It is spoken in Galicia, an area in the north-west of Spain.

• **Basque** is spoken in northern Spain, in the Basque region. Basque is a very ancient language. Unlike the other languages spoken in Spain, Basque is not derived from Latin, so it sounds completely different from the others.

Languages in Latin America

Spanish is spoken as the offical language in most of the countries of Central and South America. The only big exception is Brazil, where Portuguese is the official language. The Spanish of South and Central America is extremely varied, with lots of local dialects and accents. It developed originally from the 16th and 17th century Castilian Spanish of southern Spain, so it has some general similarities (the letter *c*, for example, is not lisped anywhere in Latin America). However, since the 16th century it has evolved completely separately from the Spanish of Spain.

Latin American countries have their own local languages as well, and these often influence how Spanish is spoken (see right for more details).

96

Spanish in Latin America

Spanish is the official language of the 19 Latin American countries listed below:

1 Argentina (*Argentina*)
2 Bolivia (*Bolivia*)
3 Chile (*Chile*)
4 Colombia (*Colombia*)
5 Costa Rica (*Costa Rica*)
6 Cuba (*Cuba*)
7 Dominican Republic (*República Dominicana*)
8 Ecuador (*Ecuador*)
9 El Salvador (*El Salvador*)
10 Guatemala (*Guatemala*)
11 Honduras (*Honduras*)
12 Mexico (*Méjico*)
13 Nicaragua (*Nicaragua*)
14 Panama (*Panamá*)
15 Paraguay (*Paraguay*)
16 Peru (*Perú*)
17 Puerto Rico (*Puerto Rico*)
18 Uruguay (*Uruguay*)
19 Venezuela (*Venezuela*)

Local words and expressions

Spain colonised Latin America in the 16th century. Since then, the countries in Latin America have all become independent from Spain. However, Spanish is still the official language of most of them. Latin American Spanish uses a lot of local words and expressions, some of which come from local indigenous languages. Here are some examples:

• In the Andes (Colombia, Ecuador, Bolivia and Peru), lots of people speak a language called Quechua as their first language, so Andean Spanish is peppered with Quechuan words. You might hear somebody talking about *choclo* (corn), *chakra* (a field), or *rocoto* (a kind of hot pepper).
The word *Llama* (which is the name of a kind of Latin American animal) is originally a Quechua word. It is used in lots of different languages, including Spanish and English.

• The word *chocolate* (chocolate) is originally a Nahuatl word. Nahuatl was the language spoken by the Aztecs, a tribe living in Mexico when the Spanish first arrived there in the 16th century.

• The word *catire* is a word which originated in the Caribbean. It is used in Venezuela to describe somebody with fair hair.

Spanish pronunciation guide

Pronunciation is how words sound. In Spanish, many letters are not said in the same way as in English. Spanish also has groups of letters that are said in a special way.

The list below shows you how letters and groups of letters are usually said. Letters missing from the list sound the same or nearly the same as in English. Bear in mind, though, that there are exceptions and also that people say things differently depending on where they come from.

Learn these tips little by little and try out the words given as examples. If you can get a Spanish speaker to help you, ask them to make the sounds and say the words so that you can copy what you hear.

Vowel sounds

a sounds like "a" in "cat", for example when used in *casa* and *una*.

e sounds like "e" in "let", for example in *el*, *le* and *torre*. Unlike an English "e", it is never silent.

i sounds like "i" in "machine", but shorter, for example in *camino*.

o sounds like "o" in "hot", for example in *alto* or *toro*.

u sounds like "oo" in "root", for example in *un* and *una*.

Groups of vowels

When you have two or more vowels together in Spanish, you usually pronounce each vowel in turn.
e.g. **eu** is said "e/oo" as in *Europa*.
iu is said "ee/oo", as in *ciudad*.
ie is said "ee/e", as in *comiendo*.

The same thing applies when you have double vowels.
e.g. **ee** is said "e/e", as in *leer*.

Vowels with *g* and *q* words

Spanish words beginning with a "g" or "q", are sometimes followed by "ue" or "ui". This pattern also sometimes appears in the middle of words. Usually, the "u" in these words is silent:
e.g. *guerra* (war)
quirófano (operating theatre)

However, sometimes the u is stressed (ü). In these cases it is always pronounced:
e.g. *pingüino* (penguin)
piragüismo (canoeing)

Lisping

In some areas of Spain, people lisp certain letters. This sounds almost exactly like the "th" sound in the English word "thing". The letters which are lisped are "c" and "z". "C" is only lisped if it comes before certain letters (see p. 99). Lisping is common in Castilian Spanish (see page 96), but it is not done in southern Spain, or anywhere in Latin America.

Consonants

c is said as in "cat", for example in *casa*. However, before "i" or "e", it is lisped, and sounds like the "th" in "thing", for example in *cine* and *cesta*.

ch sounds like "ch" in "cheese", for example in *chico*.

g is like in "good", for example in *gato*. However, before "e" or "i", it sounds like "ch" in the Scottish word "loch", or a bit like the "h" in "hate", for example in *coger* and *girar*. When "g" is followed by "ue" or "ui", the "u" is not sounded but it makes the "g" sound in "good", for example in *guerra* and *guitarra* (see previous page for more about this).

h is not sounded at all, for example in *hola*.

j is said like "ch" in the Scottish word "loch", or a bit like the "h" in "hate", for example in *jardín*. It is the same sound as **g** before "e" or "i" (see above).

ll sounds like the "y" in "yes", but with a hint of an "l" sound in front of it (a bit like the "llia" in "brilliant"), for example in *llave*.

ñ is like the "ni(o)" sound in "onion", for example *mañana* and *año*. The sign that goes over the "n" to make it sound like this is called a tilde.

qu sounds like the "c" in "cat", for example in *pequeño*. It is the same sound as the c in *casa* (see above). qu is always followed by "e" or "i".

When **r** comes between two vowels in the middle of a word, it is an "r" sound made by putting your tongue on the ridge just behind your top teeth, for example in *pero*. When **r** is at the beginning of a word or comes after n, or when you have **rr** in a word, the "r" sound is virtually trilled (your tongue is in the same position but you make it vibrate), for example in *ropa* and *perro*.

s sounds like the "s" in "same", for example in *cansado*. However, before "b", "d", "g", "l", "m" and "n", it sounds like the "s" in "trousers", for example in *desde* and *mismo*.

v sounds like the "b" in "bad", for example in *viejo*. That's why the "v" in *Valencia* and the "b" in *Barcelona* sound the same.

y sounds like the "y" in "yes", for example in *yo*. However, when it is used on its own, as a word (to mean "and"), it sounds like the Spanish "i" (like the "i" in "machine").

z sounds like the "th" in "thing", for example in *zapatillas*. It is the same sound as a **c** before "e" or "i" (see **c** above left).

💻 Internet links

For links to websites where you can listen to examples of Spanish pronunciation, or try a random idiom generator to improve your spoken Spanish, go to **www.usborne-quicklinks.com**

99

Speech bubble key: chapters 1 to 5

Chapter 1

• *¡Mira, Fede!* Fede, look!
• *Es la costa.* It's the coast!
• *¡Sí! Y también hay una ciudad.* Oh yes! There's a town too.
• *Es un puerto.* It's a port.
• *¡Un río!* A river!
• *¡Y un lago!* And a lake!
• *¡Un pueblo!* A village!
• *¡Ay va, montañas!* Oh, mountains!
• *¡Mira! Eso es Villatorres.* Look! It's Villatorres.
• *Sí, ahí hay los puentes...* Yes, there are the bridges...
• *...y las dos torres.* ...and the two towers.
• *¡Ahí está el aeropuerto!* There's the airport!
• *¡Qué bien! ¡Caramelos!* Great! Sweets!
• *¿Qué es eso, Carmen?* What's that, Carmen?
• *Es el mapa.* It's the map.
• *Y aquí está la casa Salchicha.* And here's the Salchicha house.
• *Ah, la casa Salchicha...* Ah, the Salchicha house...

Chapter 2

• *Tengo un bolso negro pequeño.* I've got a small black bag.
• *¡Eh, Fede! También tienes una tienda.* Hey, Fede! You've got a tent as well.
• *¡Ah, sí! Tengo una tienda verde.* Oh yes! I've got a green tent.
• *¡Oh, perdón!* Oh, sorry!
• *¡Qué alto!* How tall!
• *Uf... Estoy cansada...* Phew... I'm tired...
• *Una maleta verde, un bolso azul...* A green suitcase... a blue bag...
• *Tengo un bolso azul.* I've got a blue bag.
• *Gracias, es muy amable.* Thank you, you are so kind.
• *Hola ¿María? Soy Carmen.* Hello María? It's Carmen.
• *Estamos en Villatorres.* We're in Villatorres.
• *Está bien, tenemos tu mapa.* It's alright, we have your map.
• *Éste es tu bolso.* This is your bag.
• *No, es su bolso.* No it's not, it's his bag.
• *Mi mochila es roja.* My backpack is red.
• *Mis maletas son grises.* My suitcases are grey.
• *Aquí está su maleta, señorita.* Here's your suitcase, Miss.

Chapter 3

• *Andas muy despacio.* You're walking very slowly.
• *No, miro el paisaje.* No, I'm looking at the countryside.
• *¡Ah, sí! El sol brilla...* Oh yes, the sun's shining...
• *...y los pájaros cantan.* ...and the birds are singing.
• *Perdón, buscamos el camping.* Excuse me, we're looking for the campsite.
• *Eso es fácil, es todo recto.* That's easy. It's straight ahead.
• *Quiero una mesa a la sombra.* I want a table in the shade.
• *Quiero un zumo de naranja muy frío.* I want a very cold orange juice.

- *Yo quisiera un zumo de manzana.* I'd like an apple juice.
- *Y yo quisiera una coca-cola, por favor.* And I'd like a Coke, please.
- *Quisiera pagar, por favor.* I'd like to pay, please.
- *¿Qué queréis hacer ahora?* What would you like to do now?
- *Queremos alquilar unas bicicletas.* We want to hire some bikes.

The mysterious letter:
A desert island, 1893
My dear son Santiago, I am an old man. I am alone on a desert island, and my house near Villatorres is empty. I have a secret. I am very rich. Now my treasure is your treasure. My house hides the first clue. First of all you look for the two ships. Farewell, Sancho Salchicha

Chapter 4

- *¡Buenos días! Somos los amigos de María.* Hello. We're María's friends.
- *¡Buenos días! Yo soy su madre.* Hello. I'm her mother.
- *Me llamo Alicia... y este es nuestro perro Guau Guau.* My name's Alicia... and here is our dog, Guau Guau.
- *¿De quién es el gato?* Whose is the cat?
- *Es de María. Se llama Kiti.* He's María's. His name's Kiti.
- *Aquí está la habitación de mis padres... mi habitación y... la habitación del huésped.* Here's my parents' bedroom... my room and... the lodger's room.
- *Aquí está el estudio de mi madre.* Here's my mother's studio.
- *Aquí escondemos todos los tesoros de la familia.* Here we hide all the family treasures.
- *Ese es un cuadro muy viejo de la casa Salchicha.* Here's an old painting of the Salchicha house.
- *Y ese es un retrato antiguo del abuelo de María, Santiago.* That's a portrait of María's grandfather, Santiago.
- *¡Oh, no! Es Comelotodo, la cabra de los vecinos. Se come cualquier cosa.* Oh no! It's Comelotodo, the neighbours' goat. He'll eat anything!
- *¿De quién es esa ropa?* Whose are these clothes?
- *Es de mi hermano...* They're my brother's...
- *¿Y estos prismáticos?* And these binoculars?
- *Son tambien de Fede.* They're Fede's as well.
- *Me gustan estas gafas.* I like these glasses.
- *Son de Carmen.* They're Carmen's.

Chapter 5

- *¡Cuidado! Ve despacio.* Careful! Go slowly.
- *Tranquila, Comelotodo.* Keep calm, Comelotodo.
- *Lanza la cuerda.* Throw the rope.
- *Sé bueno, Guau Guau.* Be good, Guau Guau.
- *¡Cuidado!* Watch out!
- *¡Venga! ¡Tirad!* Go on! Pull!
- *¡Rápido, la puerta!* Quick, the gate!

Chapters 5 to 9

- *¡Date prisa!* Hurry!
- *Tenéis que visitar todo - la iglesia antigua, las cuevas, Puerto Viejo...* You must visit everything - the old church, the caves, Puerto Viejo...
- *Yo tengo que hacer compras en Puerto Viejo.* I must do some shopping in Puerto Viejo.
- *¡Hasta luego!* See you later!
- *Hay que cerrar la puerta.* You have to shut the gate.
- *Tuerce a la izquierda... y sigue el primer camino a la derecha.* Turn left... and take the first path on the right.
- *¡Guau Guau, ven aquí!* Guau Guau, come here!
- *Esta debe de ser la casa Salchicha.* This must be the Salchicha house.
- *Hay que encontrar esa pista rápidamente.* I have to find that clue quickly.
- *En primer lugar tengo que buscar mi lima.* First I must look for my nail file.
- *¡Cállate!* Shut up!
- *Estas cerraduras deben de ser muy viejas.* These locks must be very old.

Chapter 6

- *Buenas tardes, señora Salchicha.* Good evening, Mrs Salchicha.
- *¡Hola!* Hello.
- *¿Tiene usted manzanas?* Do you have any apples?
- *¿Lleva una cesta?* Do you have a basket?
- *Quisiera dos kilos de naranjas.* I'd like two kilos of oranges.
- *¿A qué hora abre la farmacia?* What time does the pharmacy open?
- *No lo sé. La señora Pastilla está enferma.* I don't know. Mrs Pastilla is unwell.
- *Perdón, ¿dónde está la panadería?* Excuse me, where is the bakery?
- *¿Qué es eso?* What is that?
- *Es un cangrejo.* It's a crab.
- *¿Cuánto valen estos pasteles?* How much do these cakes cost?
- *¿Cuántos pasteles quiere usted?* How many cakes do you want?
- *¿Qué quieres?* What do you want?
- *Quiero un helado.* I want an ice cream.
- *¿Qué buscas Carmen?* What are you looking for, Carmen?
- *¿Dónde está? ¡Ah!* Where is it? Ah!
- *María, ¿me puedes explicar esta carta?* María, can you explain this letter?
- *¿Es una broma?* Is it a joke?
- *¡Qué bien! ¡Es la búsqueda del tesoro de verdad!* Great! A real treasure hunt!

Chapter 7

- *La puerta no está cerrada con llave.* The door isn't locked.
- *Pero las bicicletas no están ahí...* But the bikes aren't there...
- *¡Silencio, Guau Guau! No hay que ladrar tan fuerte.* Be quiet, Guau Guau! You mustn't bark so loud!
- *¿Qué buscas?* What are you looking for?
- *No hay nadie...* There isn't anyone here...
- *¡Hay un ladrón en la casa!* There's a burglar in the house!
- *¿Qué barcos? No veo ningun barco.* What ships? I can't see any ships.
- *¡Buenas noches, Pedro! ¡Hola Juan!* Good evening, Pedro. Hello, Juan.

- *Buenas noches, Alicia. ¡Oh no! No hay ninguna aspirina.* Good evening, Alicia. Oh no! There aren't any aspirins.
- *Sí, ya lo sé. Es porque la farmacia está cerrada.* Yes, I know. The pharmacy is closed.
- *No tengo nada, no tengo aspirinas, no tengo esparadrapo...* I haven't got anything, no aspirins, no plasters...
- *¡Hola a todo el mundo!* Hi, everyone!
- *¡Oh, no!, y aún no tengo la pista.* Oh, no! And I still don't have the clue.
- *Aquí están los dos barcos.* Here are the two ships.
- *¡Ay va! Hay un hombre afuera.* Hey! There's a man outside.
- *María, ¿quién es ese hombre?* María, who's that man?
- *No sé.* I don't know.
- *No es Juan, el huésped...* It's not Juan, the lodger...
- *¿Dónde estabais? La cena está lista.* Where are you? Supper's ready.
- *Vale, mamá. Un momento.* OK Mum. One minute.
- *¡Mirad! No son exactamente iguales.* Look! They're not exactly the same.

Chapter 8

- *Vamos al supermercado, cariño.* Let's go to the supermarket, darling.
- *¡Silencio! Estoy leyendo el periódico.* Quiet! I'm reading my newspaper.
- *¿A qué hora empieza la película?* What time does the film start?
- *¿A qué hora vuelve a casa esta noche?* What time are you coming home this evening?
- *¡Qué bien huele!* What a great smell!
- *Quisiera queso.* I want cheese.
- *¿Te gustan las hamburguesas?* Do you like hamburgers?
- *Sí, pero prefiero el filete.* Yes, but I prefer steak.
- *¡Agh! ¡Qué mala está la ensalada!* Yuk! What bad salad this is!
- *¿Qué hacen esos niños?* What are those kids doing?
- *¿Y por qué sacan fotos?* And why are they taking photos?
- *Cuidado, trae la sopa.* Watch out, he's bringing some soup.
- *¡Bueno, ya basta! Salid ahora mismo.* Right, that's enough! Get out this instant!
- *¡Va, venga!* Hey, come on!
- *¡Mirad, tengo la próxima pista!* Look! I've got the next clue.

Chapter 9

- *¡Mirad por la ventana!* Look through the window!
- *Cerca de la salida... junto a la mujer alta.* Near the exit... next to the tall woman.
- *¡Es el hombre del aeropuerto!* It's the man from the airport!
- *¡Es el hombre de la carta!* It's the man with the letter!
- *¡Es el hombre del jardín!* It's the man from the garden!
- *¡Es el mismo hombre!* It's the same man!
- *¡Rápido! Debe de querer nuestro tesoro.* Quickly! He must want our treasure.
- *¡Oh no! ¡El hombre calvo! Allí delante de la fuente.* Oh no! The bald man! Over there in front of the fountain.

Chapters 9 to 12

- *Viene por el muelle.* He's coming onto the quay.
- *¡De prisa, venid detrás de esta red!* Quick, come behind this net!
- *¡Está bien!* It's OK!
- *Vale, pon la nota y las fotos en este banco.* Right, put the note and the photos on this bench.
- *¿Tienes una lupa?* Do you have a magnifying glass?
- *Sí, pero está en casa.* Yes, but at home.
- *Podemos ir a casa de mi compañero, Rafa. Vive enfrente de la estación.* We can go to my friend Rafa's house. He lives opposite the station.
- *Sí, tengo una lupa. Está encima de la mesa en el desván.* Yes, I've got a magnifying glass. It's on the table in the attic.

The note:
The next clue is in a building in Puerto Viejo. Find the answers to these questions: Where is the dog? Where is the bench? Where is the cow? Where is the farm?

Chapter 10

- *¿Por qué os escondéis?* Why are you hiding?
- *Porque no nos gusta el colegio.* Because we don't like school.
- *¿Qué hora es?* What's the time?
- *Son las ocho, señorita.* It's eight o'clock, Miss.
- *¿Y ahora?* And now?
- *Son las nueve y cuarto.* It's quarter past nine.
- *Gaspar, ¿a qué hora te levantas?* Gaspar, what time do you get up?
- *A las siete y media.* At half past seven.
- *¿Te vistes solo?* Do you get dressed on your own?
- *Claro.* Of course.
- *No me siento bien.* I don't feel well.
- *¡No es nada, cálmate!* It's nothing serious, calm down!
- *¡Mira! Es el lápiz de color que falta.* Look! It's the crayon that's missing.
- *¡Eh! Ese dibujo que tienes es de Manuel.* Hey! That's Miguel's drawing you've got.
- *Mira esa foto antigua.* Look at that old photo.
- *¡Ay va! Esa debe ser la pista que buscamos.* Oh! That must be the clue we're looking for.
- *El hombre que corta la cinta es Sancho Salchicha.* The man who's cutting the ribbon is Sancho Salchicha.
- *Y esta es la señal que aparece en todas sus pistas.* And there's the sign that's on all his clues.
- *Podemos volver esta tarde.* We can come back this evening.
- *¡Buena idea!* Good idea!

Chapter 11

- *¿Quién es usted? ¿Qué está haciendo aquí?* Who are you? What are you doing here?
- *Eh... soy el técnico, estoy arreglando la fotocopiadora.* Er... I'm the mechanic. I'm mending the photocopier.
- *Sí, estoy envolviendo una pieza que está rota.* Yes. I'm just wrapping up a broken part.

104

- *Entonces, ¿funciona bien ahora?* So, it's working OK now?
- *Eh, sí...* Er, yes...
- *¿Puedo cerrar, señor López?* Can I close up, Mr López?
- *Sí, claro.* Yes, of course.
- *¿Qué podemos hacer para entrar?* What do we do to get in?
- *¡Venid por aquí!* Come this way!
- *¿Qué estás haciendo, Carmen?* What are you doing, Carmen?
- *No seas tonto. Estoy buscando la foto...* Don't be stupid. I'm looking for the photo...
- *¡Demasiado tarde! El hombre calvo tiene la pista.* Too late! The bald man's got the clue.
- *¿Cómo lo sabes?* How do you know?
- *Porque ése es su maletín.* Because that's his briefcase.
- *Bien, debemos ir a la comisaría.* Right, we'll have to go to the police station.
- *Está cerrada.* It's closed!
- *Bueno, tendremos que volver mañana por la mañana.* Right, we must come back tomorrow morning.
- *¿Conoces al policía?* Do you know the policeman?
- *Sí, es bastante simpatíco.* Yes, he's quite nice.

Chapter 12

- *¿Qué hacemos con el maletín?* What do we do with the briefcase?
- *¿Se lo enseñamos a tus padres?* Do we show it to your parents?
- *No, no debemos enseñárselo.* No, we mustn't show it to them.
- *Primero debemos contárselo todo a la policía.* First we must tell the police everything.
- *La cena está lista.* Supper's ready.
- *Lo puedo esconder en mi tienda de campaña.* I can hide it in my tent.
- *¡Buena idea!* Good idea!
- *El hombre calvo tiene la pista del colegio.* The bald man's got the clue from the school.
- *Para encontrarla, hay que buscar al hombre calvo.* To find it, we have to find the bald man.
- *Su dirección puede estar en el maletín.* His address might be in his briefcase.
- *Acercaos.* Come next to me.
- *Carmen, pásale mi linterna a María.* Carmen, pass my torch to María.
- *Una agenda, un periódico...* A diary, a newspaper...
- *¡Mirad! Debajo hay pedazos de papel.* Look! Underneath there are some bits of paper.
- *Es un postal en trozos pequeños.* It's a postcard in small pieces.
- *Pero, ¿la podemos leer?* But can we read it?

The postcard jigsaw:

Querido Ramón: gracias por tu carta. Sí, Antonio y Ana Campos viven cerca de Villatorres. Me pides su dirección. Aquí está: La Granja de los Tres Robles, Carretera del Puente Nuevo, cerca de Puerto Viejo. ¿Pero por qué Villatorres? No es un pueblo muy apasionante. De todas formas, tienen un habitación para ti y yo te los recomiendo. La casa es tranquila y la comida es buena. Bueno, buen viaje. Isabel

Chapters 12 to 16

Dear Ramón, Thank you for your letter. Yes, Antonio and Ana Campos live near Villatorres. You ask me for their address. Here it is: the Tres Robles farm, Carreterra del Puente Nuevo, near Puerto Viejo. But why Villatorres? It's not a very exciting town. Anyhow, they probably have a room for you and I recommend them to you. It's quiet at their place and you eat well. So, have a good journey. Isabel

Chapter 13

- *Entonces, ¿dónde estaba este maletín?* So, where was this briefcase?
- *Estaba encima de la fotocopiadora del colegio.* It was on the school photocopier.
- *¿Y por qué estabais vosotros allí?* And why were you there?
- *Porque estamos buscando un tesoro...* Because we're looking for treasure...
- *...y había una pista en el colegio.* ...and there was a clue in the school.
- *¿Qué tesoro?* What treasure?
- *Es de mi familia.* It belongs to my family.
- *Ah, ya entiendo, y este estafador lo quiere robar...* Ah, I see, and this crook wants to steal it...
- *¡Exactamente! La pista es una foto antigua.* Exactly! The clue is an old photo.
- *Ayer por la noche la foto ya no estaba allí...* Last night the photo wasn't there any more...
- *...pero encontramos el maletín del estafador.* ...but we found the crook's briefcase.
- *Probablamente es el maletín de un profesor.* It's most probably one of the teacher's.
- *No, el estefador lo tenía antes.* No, the crook had it before.
- *¡Ya basta! Regresad a casa.* That's enough! Go home.
- *Devuelve este maletín al colegio ahora mismo.* Take this briefcase back to school right now.
- *¡Qué le vamos a hacer! Tendremos que seguir sin la policía.* Too bad! We'll have to carry on without the police.
- *Afortunadamente sabemos la dirección del hombre calvo.* Luckily we know the bald man's address.
- *¡Eh, mirad! Todavía tengo la agenda que estaba en el maletín.* Oh look! I've still got the diary that was in the briefcase!
- *Estaba en mi bolsillo.* It was in my pocket.

Chapter 14

- *¿Qué es eso?* What's that?
- *Estaba en la agenda.* It was in the diary.
- *Parece interesante...* It looks interesting...

The magazine cutting:
Rare birds on the Lorazul islands. A hundred years ago, there were many blue parrots on the Lorazul islands. The inhabitants worshipped them and built temples to them. These birds are now very rare and it is forbidden to catch any. Last year, you could sometimes see some on Kuku, a remote desert island.

The message:
Mr Robón, Find me a pair of blue parrots for my collection.
Your fee: 15.000 euros. Mrs Buitre.

- *¡Eh! Las islas Lorazul... mi bisabuelo iba a menudo allí para estudiar las plantas.*
  Hey! The Lorazul islands... My great-grandfather often went there to study plants.
- *Era botánico...* He was a botanist...
- *Y el hombre calvo estaba en esas islas para robar loros.* And the bald man was
  on those islands to steal some parrots.
- *Venid, os quiero enseñar una cosa en casa.* Come on, I want to show you
  something at home.

The letter:
Sir, Sadly, your father is very probably dead. He knew our islands well, but at the
time of his disappearance, he was looking for plants on some dangerous and very
remote islands. He was with two botanist friends. They had a good boat, but it was
the stormy season. Pedro Peperoni, Governor of the island

Chapter 15

- *La comida está casi lista.* Lunch is nearly ready.
- *¿Compraste pan?* Did you bring back any bread?
- *¡Oh, no! ¡Lo siento, se me olvidé!* Oh no sorry, I forgot!
- *No importa* It doesn't matter.
- *Hay que esperar a papá. Fue a una reunión que se termina a las dos.* We'll have
  to wait for Dad... He went to a meeting that finishes at two.
- *¿Tienes la agenda?* Have you got the diary?
- *No, la dejé en mi tienda de campaña. Esperad aquí.* No, I put it in my tent. Wait here!
- *Oh... Aquí explica cómo encontró la carta de Sancho Salchicha.* Oh... It explains
  how he found Sancho Salchicha's letter.
- *Buscaba loros azules.* He was looking for blue parrots.
- *Logró llegar a la isla Kuku...* He managed to get to Kuku island...
- *...A la entrada de una cueva, vio un cofre viejo.* At the entrance to a
  cave, he saw an old chest.
- *Dentro encontró una carta que hablaba de un tesoro.* Inside he found a letter
  that talked about treasure.
- *Sí, la carta que robó...* Yes, the letter that he stole...
- *¡Venid a comer!, papá está aquí.* Come and sit down! Here's Dad.
- *Lo siento, pero la reunión fue muy larga.* Sorry, but I had a very long meeting...

Chapter 16

- *Tenemos que ir a la Granja de las Tres Robles...* We must go to the Tres Robles farm...
- *...para encontrar al señor Robón y la pista del colegio.* ...to find Mr. Robón and
  the clue from the school.
- *¿Café, señor Robón?* Some coffee, Mr. Robón?
- *Gracias... Em, quería hacerles una pregunta...* Thank you...
  Er, I wanted to ask you...
- *Esta mañana estuve en Villatorres.* I went to Villatorres this morning.
- *Vi el castillo y las dos torres...* I saw the castle and the two towers...
- *...pero no pude encontrar la torre en ruinas.*
  ...but I couldn't find the ruined tower.

- *¿Por qué quiere verla? Solamente hay piedras viejas.* Why do you want to see it? There are only a few old stones.
- *Er... Me gustan las ruinas.* Er... I like ruins...
- *Vale, ¿fue al parque?* Well, did you go to the park?
- *Sí, pero no vi nada.* Yes, but I didn't see anything there.
- *¡Ah! Usted no bajó hasta el río...* Ah! You didn't go right down to the river.
- *Ah Antonia, estás ya despierta.* Ah Antonia, you're up already.
- *...sí, la torre en ruinas está al lado del río.* ...Yes, the ruined tower is by the river.
- *¿Ah, sí? Muy interesante...* Oh, really? Very interesting...
- *La próxima pista debe estar en la torre vieja.* The next clue must be at the old tower.

Chapter 17

- *Entonces, ha descifrado la pista del colegio...* So he's worked out the clue from the school...
- *...y ahora quiere ir a la torre en ruinas.* ...And now he wants to go to the ruined tower.
- *Pero todavía no la ha encontrado.* But he hasn't found it yet.
- *Entonces, tenemos que ir allí ahora mismo, para llegar antes que él.* So we must go there straight away, before him.
- *Necesitamos las bicis.* We need the bikes.
- *La verdad es que nunca he explorado la torre porque hay una valla.* I've never really explored the tower because there's a fence.
- *¡Nada! He buscado por todas partes y he examinado cada piedra.* Nothing! I've looked everywhere and examined each stone.
- *¡Eh! He encontrado algo aquí.* Hey! I've found something here.
- *¡Mirad... es la señal de Sancho Salchicha!*
  Look... It's Sancho Salchicha's sign!

The writing on the tower:
We have kept this ruined tower because it is a sacred monument for the inhabitants of Villatorres. The pirates of Pirate Island destroyed it three years ago, but now, we have got our revenge. We have won our last battle against them, we have expelled them from their fort on the island and they have disappeared from our country.

Chapter 18

- *Entonces, tenemos que ir a la Isla de los Piratas.* So we must go to Pirate Island.
- *Hoy no. Llegaremos demasiado tarde...* Not today. We'll get there too late...
- *Pero el hombre encontrará la pista aquí e... irá a la isla de noche.* But the man will find the clue here and... he might go to the island during the night.
- *Bien, tenemos que esconder esta pista con hojas. ¡Ahí!* Well, we must hide this clue with leaves. There!
- *También podemos dejar un rastro falso.*
  We can also leave a false trail.

- *¡Buena idea! Se irá por otro camino y no nos molestará.* Brilliant! He'll go off in the wrong direction and won't disturb us.
- *Bien, debemos dejarle una nota* Right, we must leave him a note.
- *Tengo una buena idea.* I've got a good idea.
- *¿Pero dónde la esconderemos?* But where shall we hide it?
- *Fede y yo podemos buscar un buen sitio* Fede and I can look for a good place.
- *Podemos esconderla aquí y dibujar su señal.* We can hide the note here and draw his sign.
- *¡Qué buena idea! Seguro que caerá en la trampa.* What a great idea! He'll definitely fall for it.

The false trail:

Querido hijo: Ahora has encontrado todas las pistas que he dejado. Aquí esta tu última misión. Será difícil. Tendrás que ir a la comisaría de Puerto Viejo. Verás una ventana sin barrotes. Entrarás por allí. Dentro encontrarás una pared con paneles de madera. Todas mis joyas y mi fortuna están allí. Adiós S.S.

My dear son: Now you have found all the clues I left. Here is your last task. It will be difficult. You will have to go to the police station in Puerto Viejo. You will see one window without bars. You will go in that way. Inside you will find one wall with wooden panels. All my jewels and my fortune are there. Farewell. S.S.

Chapter 19

- *Vamos a cerrar...* We're going to close up...
- *Muy bien, voy a ordenar las cosas...* Fine. I'll just tidy things up.
- *¡Eh! Es el hombre de la foto que los chicos me enseñaron...* Hey, it's the man from the picture that those children showed me.
- *Sí, es el mismo hombre.* Yes, it's the same man.
- *¡Hola! ¿Madrid? Quisiera saber los datos del número 7454.* Hello! Madrid? I'd like details on number 7454.
- *Bien, voy a buscarlos y después se los enviaré por fax.* Right, I'll go and get them and then I'll fax them to you.
- *De acuerdo, gracias.* All right. Thanks!
- *¡Ah, es ésta! Todas las demás tienen barrotes.* Ah, it's this one. Those all have bars.
- *Vale, no será muy difícil. Podré romper la ventana.* Right, it won't be very difficult. I'll be able to break the window pane.
- *Primero, voy a cenar y volveré después. Será muy de noche.* First I'll go and have supper. I'll come back later when it's really dark.
- *Ah, por fin...* Ah, at last...
- *Bien, mañana iré a la casa Salchicha.* Right, tomorrow I'll go to the Salchicha house.
- *Probablemente los chicos podrán ayudarme a encontrarlo.* The children will probably be able to help me find him.
- *¿Pero qué ha sido eso?* Oh! What was that?
- *¡Es él! ¡Eh... Alto! Queda usted detenido.*
  It's him! Hey... Stop... You're under arrest.

Chapters 20 to 22

Chapter 20

- *¿Me puedes prestar tu toalla?* Can you lend me your towel?
- *¡Agh! Está tan mojada como la mía.* Yuk! It's as wet as mine.
- *¡Hola, Rafa! ¿Tienes tu barca aquí?* Hi, Rafa! Have you got your boat here?
- *Sí, está allí.* Yes, it's over there.
- *¿Nos la prestas? Queremos ir a la Isla de los Piratas.* Can we borrow it? We want to go to Pirate Island.
- *Sí, claro. Es la más pequeña.* Yes, of course. It's the smallest.
- *¡Cuidado! Uno de los remos es más corto que el otro.* Watch out! One of the oars is shorter than the other.
- *Eh! Estamos empezando a hacer círculos.* Hey! We're starting to go around in circles.
- *Sí. ¡Fede! No estás remando tan de prisa como yo.* Yes, Fede! You're not rowing as fast as me.
- *Es que tú tienes el mejor remo.* It's because you've got the best oar.
- *No, soy más fuerte que tú.* No, I'm stronger than you!
- *Ahí está el fuerte.* There's the fort.
- *Es más viejo que la torre en ruinas..* It's even older than the ruined tower.
- *Hay muchos calabozos y túneles...* It's got lots of dungeons and tunnels...
- *...pero no se puede bajar ahí.* ...but you can't go down there.
- *¡Qué raro! La puerta suele estar cerrada.* That's odd, normally the gate's shut.
- *¡Eh, id más despacio!* Hey, go more slowly!
- *¡Oh, no!* Oh, no!
- *Mirad, hay cuatro túneles.* Look, there are four tunnels.
- *¡No!* No!
- *¡Ahora no podemos salir!* Now we can't get out!
- *¡Venid aquí! ¡Mirad!* Come here! Look at this!
- *Mi túnel no es tan largo como el tuyo.* My tunnel isn't as long as yours.
- *Mi primer túnel era tan largo como el tuyo, pero mi segundo túnel es más corto.* My first tunnel was as long as yours, but my second one is shorter.
- *El mío es más largo que el primer túnel de Carmen.* Mine is longer than Carmen's first one.

Chapter 21

- *Si el tesoro está aquí, lo encontraremos.* If the treasure is here, we'll find it!
- *¡No hay nada! El túnel se termina aquí.* Nothing! The tunnel ends here.
- *¿Verías mejor si llevaras la linterna?* Would you see better if you had the torch?
- *Sí, ¡pásamela!* Yes, pass it to me!
- *¡Vaya! Hay una anilla de hierro en la pared! ¿Qué pasará si tiro de ella?* Oh! There's an iron ring in the wall! What'll happen if I pull it?
- *¡Aaah!* Aaah!
- *¡Hola! Quisiera hablar con María, Carmen y Fede.* Hello! I'd like to talk to María, Carmen and Fede.
- *Me gustaría darles las gracias. Me ayudaron a atrapar a un estafador.* I'd like to thank them. They helped me to catch a crook!
- *¿Querría esperarles?* Would you like to wait for them?
- *No, ya volveré, no quisiera molestarles.* No, I'll come back. I wouldn't want to disturb you.

- *Pero primero, tal vez usted podría contarnos la historia. No sabemos nada.* But first you could perhaps tell us the story. We know nothing about it.

Chapter 22

- *¡Rápido! Tenemos que buscar una salida..* Quick! We must look for a way out...
- *Seguramente encontraremos una, si volvemos a los escalones.* Surely we'll find one if we go back to the steps.
- *¡Mirad! ¡Luz!* Look! Light!
- *¡Uf!* Phew!
- *Carmen, si mueves esas piedras, nadie podrá ver la entrada...* Carmen, if you move those rocks, nobody'll be able to see the entrance...
- *¡Le podré regalar a Rafa un par de remos nuevos!* I'm going to be able to treat Rafa to a new pair of oars!

María's letter:
Villatorres, Monday 2 September
Dear Fede and Carmen: Here's the article from the Voice of Villatorres that tells our story. It's brilliant! What are you going to do with your share of the reward? I'm going to buy a CD player with mine. If your Mum agrees, I'll come to your place during the Christmas holidays, so see you soon I hope! Love, María.

The newspaper article:
The Salchicha family treasure.

María Salchicha with her friends Fede and Carmen Molinero and her dog, Guau Guau.
Ramon Robón, the rare bird thief who wanted to steal the Salchicha family treasure.

María Salchicha and her friends Fede and Carmen have had an exciting August: they found some treasure and helped the police to catch a crook, Ramón Robón. A few months ago, Robón went to the Lorazul islands because he wanted to steal some endangered parrots. There he came across a letter in an old chest, that María's great-grandfather Sancho had written to his son, Santiago. Robón read the letter and set off on a hunt for the treasure. It brought him to Villatorres where he lost the letter. It ended up in the hands of Fede and Carmen, who were coming to spend a few days with their friend María. The three teenagers followed the clues from the card. They managed to find the treasure which was hidden in the Old Pirates' Fort before the robber, and helped the police to catch him.
The police have given the three children a reward of 2,000 euros. The "Voice of Villatorres" congratulates the three heroes.

Common irregular verbs: a - o

Here is a table listing the main irregular and stem-changing Spanish verbs in this book, in alphabetical order. The first column shows the infinitive of the verb, followed by the *tú* and *vosotros* imperative forms, then the past participle (pp). The second and third columns show the preterite, and future tenses of the verbs.

	Present tense	Preterite tense	Future tense
conducir (to drive) ¡conduce! ¡conducid! pp: *conducido*	yo conduzco tú conduces él/ella conduce nosotros conducimos vosotros conducís ellos conducen	yo conduje tú condujiste él/ella condujo nosotros condujimos vosotros condujisteis ellos condujeron	yo conduciré tú conducirás él/ella conducirá nosotros conduciremos vosotros conduciréis ellos conducirán
conocer (to know) ¡conoce! ¡conoced! pp: *conoocido*	yo conozco tú conoces él/ella conoce nosotros conocemos vosotros conocéis ellos conocen	yo conocí tú conociste él/ella conoció nosotros conocimos vosotros conocisteis ellos conocieron	yo conoceré tú conocerás él/ella conocerá nosotros conoceremos vosotros conoceréis ellos conocerán
construir (to build) ¡construye! ¡construid! pp: *construido*	yo construyo tú construyes él/ella construye nosotros construimos vosotros construís ellos construyen	yo construí tú construiste él/ella construyó nosotros construimos vosotros construisteis ellos construyeron	yo construiré tú construirás él/ella construirá nosotros construiremos vosotros construiréis ellos construirán
contar (to count) ¡cuenta! ¡contad! pp: *contado*	yo cuento tú cuentas él/ella cuenta nosotros contamos vosotros contáis ellos cuentan	yo conté tú contaste él/ella contó nosotros contamos vosotros contasteis ellos contaron	yo contaré tú contarás él/ella contará nosotros contaremos vosotros contaréis ellos contarán
dar (to give) ¡da! ¡dad! pp: *dado*	yo doy tú das él/ella da nosotros damos vosotros dais ellos dan	yo di tú diste él/ella dio nosotros dimos vosotros disteis ellos dieron	yo daré tú darás él/ella dará nosotros daremos vosotros daréis ellos darán

desaparecer (to disappear) ¡desaparece! ¡desapareced!	yo desaparezco
	tú desapareces
	él/ella desaparece
	nosotros
	  desaparecemos
		yo desaparecí
		tú desapareciste
		él/ella desapareció
		nosotros
		  desaparecimos
			yo desapareceré
			tú desaparecerás
			él/ella desaparecerá
			nosotros
			  desapareceremos

	Present tense	**Preterite tense**	**Future tense**
pp: *desaparecido*	vosotros desaparecéis	vosotros	vosotros
	ellos desaparecen	desaparecisteis	desapareceréis
		ellos desaparecieron	ellos desaparecerán
estar (to be)	yo estoy	yo estuve	yo estaré
¡está!	tú estás	tú estuviste	tú estarás
¡estad!	él/ella está	él/ella estuvo	él/ella estará
	nosotros estamos	nosotros estuvimos	nosotros estaremos
pp: *estado*	vosotros estáis	vosotros estuvisteis	vosotros estaréis
	ellos están	ellos estuvieron	ellos estarán
dormir (to sleep)	yo duermo	yo dormí	yo dormiré
¡duerme!	tú duermes	tú dormiste	tú dormirás
¡dormid!	él/ella duerme	él/ella durmió	él/ella dormirá
	nosotros dormimos	nosotros dormimos	nosotros dormiremos
pp: *dormido*	vosotros dormís	vosotros dormisteis	vosotros dormiréis
	ellos duermen	ellos durmieron	ellos dormirán
hacer (to do, make)	yo hago	yo hice	yo haré
¡haz!	tú haces	tú hiciste	tú harás
¡haced!	él/ella hace	él/ella hizo	él/ella hará
	nosotros hacemos	nosotros hicimos	nosotros haremos
pp: *hecho*	vosotros hacéis	vosotros hicisteis	vosotros haréis
	ellos hacen	ellos hicieron	ellos harán
ir (to go)	yo voy	yo fui	yo iré
¡ve!	tú vas	tú fuiste	tú irás
¡id!	él/ella va	él/ella fue	él/ella irá
	nosotros vamos	nosotros fuimos	nosotros iremos
pp: *ido*	vosotros vais	vosotros fuisteis	vosotros iréis
	ellos van	ellos fueron	ellos irán
oler (to smell)	yo huelo	yo olí	yo oleré
¡huele!	tú hueles	tú oliste	tú olerás
¡oled!	él/ella huele	él/ella olió	él/ella olerá
	nosotros olemos	nosotros olimos	nosotros oleremos
pp: *olido*	vosotros oléis	vosotros olisteis	vosotros oleréis
	ellos huelen	ellos olieron	ellos olerán
pedir (to request)	yo pido	yo pedí	yo pediré
¡pide!	tú pides	tú pediste	tú pedirás
¡pedid!	él/ella pide	él/ella pidió	él/ella pedirá
	nosotros pedimos	nosotros pedimos	nosotros pediremos
	vosotros pedís	vosotros pedisteis	vosotros pediréis
pp: *pedido*	ellos piden	ellos pidieron	ellos pedirán

Common irregular verbs: p - v

	Present tense	Preterite tense	Future tense

pensar (to think)
¡piensa!
¡pensad!

	yo pienso	yo pensé	yo pensaré
	tú piensas	tú pensaste	tú pensarás
	él/ella piensa	él/ella pensó	él/ella pensará
	nosotros pensamos	nosotros pensamos	nosotros pensaremos
pp: pensado	vosotros pensáis	vosotros pensasteis	vosotros pensaréis
	ellos piensan	ellos pensaron	ellos pensarán

poner (to put)
¡pon!
¡poned !

	yo pongo	yo puse	yo pondré
	tú pones	tú pusiste	tú pondrás
	él/ella pone	él/ella puso	él/ella pondrá
	nosotros ponemos	nosotros pusimos	nosotros pondremos
pp: puesto	vosotros ponéis	vosotros pusisteis	vosotros pondréis
	ellos ponen	ellos pusieron	ellos pondrán

preferir (to prefer)
¡prefiere!
¡preferid!

	yo prefiero	yo preferí	yo preferiré
	tú prefieres	tú preferiste	tú preferirás
	él/ella prefiere	él/ella prefirió	él/ella preferirá
	nosotros preferimos	nosotros preferimos	nosotros preferiremos
pp: preferido	vosotros preferís	vosotros preferisteis	vosotros preferiréis
	ellos prefieren	ellos prefirieron	ellos preferirán

querer (to want)
¡quiere!
¡quered!

	yo quiero	yo quise	yo querré
	tú quieres	tú quisiste	tú querrás
	él/ella quiere	él/ella quiso	él/ella querrá
	nosotros queremos	nosotros quisimos	nosotros querremos
	vosotros queréis	vosotros quisisteis	vosotros querréis
pp: querido	ellos quieren	ellos quisieron	ellos querrán

recordar (to remember)
¡recuerda!
¡recordad!

	yo recuerdo	yo recordé	yo recordaré
	tú recuerdas	tú recordaste	tú recordarás
	él/ella recuerda	él/ella recordó	él/ella recordará
	nosotros recordamos	nosotros recordamos	nosotros recordaremos
	vosotros recordáis	vosotros recordasteis	vosotros recordaréis
pp: recordado	ellos recuerdan	ellos recordaron	ellos recordarán

repetir (to repeat)
¡repite!
¡repetid!

	yo repito	yo repetí	yo repetiré
	tú repites	tú repetiste	tú repetirás
	él/ella repite	él/ella repitió	él/ella repetirá
	nosotros repetimos	nosotros repetimos	nosotros repetiremos
pp: repetido	vosotros repetís	vosotros repetisteis	vosotros repetiréis
	ellos repiten	ellos repitieron	ellos repetirán

saber (to know)
¡sabe!
¡sabed!

	yo sé	yo supe	yo sabré
	tú sabes	tú supiste	tú sabrás
	él/ella sabe	él/ella supo	él/ella sabrá
	nosotros sabemos	nosotros supimos	nosotros sabremos
	vosotros sabéis	vosotros supisteis	vosotros sabréis

	Present tense	**Preterite tense**	**Future tense**
pp: *sabido*	*ellos saben*	*ellos supieron*	*ellos sabrán*

salir
(to go out, leave)
¡sal!
¡salid!
pp: *salido*

	yo salgo	*yo salí*	*yo saldré*
	tú sales	*tú saliste*	*tú saldrás*
	él/ella sale	*él/ella salió*	*él/ella saldrá*
	nosotros salimos	*nosotros salimos*	*nosotros saldremos*
	vosotros salís	*vosotros salisteis*	*vosotros saldréis*
	ellos salen	*ellos salieron*	*ellos saldrán*

ser (to be)
¡sé!
¡sed!
pp: *sido*

	yo soy	*yo fui*	*yo seré*
	tú eres	*tú fuiste*	*tú serás*
	él/ella es	*él/ella fue*	*él/ella será*
	nosotros somos	*nosotros fuimos*	*nosotros seremos*
	vosotros sois	*vosotros fuisteis*	*vosotros seréis*
	ellos son	*ellos fueron*	*ellos serán*

tener (to have)
¡ten!
¡tened!
pp: *tenido*

	yo tengo	*yo tuve*	*yo tendré*
	tú tienes	*tú tuviste*	*tú tendrás*
	él/ella tiene	*él/ella tuvo*	*él/ella tendrá*
	nosotros tenemos	*nosotros tuvimos*	*nosotros tendremos*
	vosotros tenéis	*vosotros tuvisteis*	*vosotros tendréis*
	ellos tienen	*ellos tuvieron*	*ellos tendrán*

venir (to come)
¡ven!
¡venid!
pp: *venido*

	yo vengo	*yo vine*	*yo vendré*
	tú vienes	*tú viniste*	*tú vendrás*
	él/ella viene	*él/ella vino*	*él/ella vendrá*
	nosotros venimos	*nosotros vinimos*	*nosotros vendremos*
	vosotros venís	*vosotros vinisteis*	*vosotros vendréis*
	ellos vienen	*ellos vinieron*	*ellos vendrán*

ver (to see)
¡ve!
¡ved!
pp: *visto*

	yo veo	*yo vi*	*yo veré*
	tú ves	*tú viste*	*tú verás*
	él/ella ve	*él/ella vio*	*él/ella verá*
	nosotros vemos	*nosotros vimos*	*nosotros veremos*
	vosotros véis	*vosotros visteis*	*vosotros veréis*
	ellos ven	*ellos vieron*	*ellos verán*

vestir (to put on,
to wear)
¡viste!
¡vestid!
pp: *vestido*

	yo visto	*yo vestí*	*yo vestiré*
	tú vistes	*tú vestiste*	*tú vestirás*
	él/ella viste	*él/ella vistió*	*él/ella vestirá*
	nosotros vestimos	*nosotros vestimos*	*nosotros vestiremos*
	vosotros vestís	*vosotros vestisteis*	*vosotros vestiréis*
	ellos visten	*ellos vistieron*	*ellos vestirán*

Vocabulary list: a - d

Here is a list of the Spanish words used in this book, along with their English translations.

Masculine/feminine words
Words that have different forms in the masculine and feminine are listed in the masculine form followed by the feminine ending ("a"). To get the feminine form, put the feminine ending on the end of the masculine form, dropping the "o" if there is one.
e.g. alto/a

Verbs
An asterisk (*) after a verb indicates it is irregular. The most common irregular verbs are conjugated on pages 112-115.

Stem-changing verbs
Stem-changing verbs are shown with their stem change in brackets.
e.g. Volver (ue)

A
a	to, at (for time)
a menudo	often
¿a qué hora?	(at) what time?
a veces	sometimes
abandonado/a	abandoned, left
abrir	to open
el/la abuelo/a	grandfather/ grandmother
acostarse (ue)	to go to bed
adiós	goodbye
el aeropuerto	airport
afortunadamente	fortunately
afuera	outside
la agenda	diary
el agua (feminine)	water
ahí	there
ahora	now
ahora mismo	right now
al final de	at/to the end of
al lado de	by, next to
algo	something
algún / alguno/a	some
allí, allá	(over) there
alquilar	to hire, to rent
¡alto!	stop!
alto/a	tall
amable	kind, nice
amarillo/a	yellow
el/la amigo/a	friend
andar	to walk
el anillo	ring (on finger)
la anilla	ring (on a wall)
el año	year
anoche	last night
ante	before, in front of
antes	before
antiguo/a	old, antique
antipático	unpleasant/ disagreeable

aparecer	to appear
apasionante	exciting
aprender	to learn
aquel/la, aquellos/as	that, those
aquello	that one
aquí	here
el árbol	tree
arreglar	to mend
el artículo	article
así	so, in this way, like that
atrapar	to catch
aún	yet, still
ayer	yesterday
ayudar a	to help
azul	blue

B
bailar	to dance
bajar	to go down
bajo/a	short
bañar	to wash
el banco	bench, bank
el barco	ship, boat
la barca	(rowing) boat
el barrote	bar (on window)
bastante	quite, enough
la batalla	battle
beber	to drink
(muchos) besos	(lots of) kisses
la bici	bike
la bicicleta	bicycle
bien	well good, right, OK
el/la bisabuelo/a	great grandfather/ great grandmother
blanco/a	white
la boca	mouth
el bolsillo	pocket
la bolsa	bag
bonito/a	pretty (for things, not

	people)
el bosque	forest, wood
el/la botánico/a	botanist
las botas	boots
el brazo	arm
brillar	to shine
la broma	joke
buen, bueno/a	good
buen viaje	have a good trip
buenas noches	good evening/night
buenas tardes	good afternoon, hello (p.m.)
buenos días	good morning, hello (a.m.)
buscar	to look for
la búsqueda del tesoro	treasure hunt

C

la cabra	goat
caerse	to fall
el café	café, coffee
la caja	box
el calabozo	dungeon
el calcetín	sock
cállate	be quiet, shut up
la calle	street
calmarse	to calm down
calvo/a	bald
la cámara de fotos	camera
cambiarse	to get changed
el camino	path, way
la camisa	shirt
la camiseta	t-shirt, vest
el camping	campsite
el campo	field, countryside
el cangrejo	crab
cansado/a	tired
cantar	to sing
capturar	to catch
el caramelo	sweet, candy
cariño	darling
caro/a	expensive
la carretera (principal)	(main) road
la carta	letter, menu
las cartas	(playing) cards
la casa	house, home
casarse	to get married
casi	almost, nearly
el castillo	castle
la cena	supper, evening meal
cenar	to have supper
cerca de	close to
cerrado/a	closed
la cerradura	lock
cerrar (ie)	to close, to shut

la cesta	basket
el chandal	tracksuit
la chaqueta	jacket
el/la chico/a	boy/girl
el cielo	sky
el cine	cinema
la cinta	ribbon, tape
el cinturón	belt
la ciudad	city
claro	of course
la coca-cola	coca-cola, cola
el coche	car
el cofre	chest
coger	to pick up, to take
la colección	collection
el colegio	school
la colina	hill
comer	to eat
la comida	food
la comisaría	police-station
como	as, like
cómo	how
el/la compañero/a	friend
comprar	to buy
comprender	to understand
con	with
con cariño	with love
conducir*	to drive
conmigo	with me
conocer*	to know
conservar	to keep, to preserve
el/la constructor/a	builder
construir*	to build
contar (ue)	to tell, to count
contento/a	pleased, happy
contigo	with you
continuar	to continue/carry on
contra	against
correo	post/mail
correr	to run
cortar	to cut
corto/a	short
la cosa	thing
la costa	coast
costar (ue)	to cost
creer	to believe
cruzar	to cross
el cuadro	painting, picture
¿cuál?	which (one)?
cualquier cosa	anything
cuándo	when
cuánto/a	how much
cuántos/as	how many
cuarto/a	fourth
la cuerda	rope
la cueva	cave
cuidado	watch out, careful

117

Vocabulary list: d - k

D

el dado	die (pl: dice)
dar*	to give
de	of, from, by
de dónde	from where
de prisa	quick, quickly
de quién	whose
de todas formas	anyhow
de verdad	real, true
de vez en cuando	sometimes
debajo de	under, underneath
deber	to have to, must
decir	to say
defender	to defend
dejar	to leave (behind)
delante de	in front of
delgado/a	thin
demasiado	too much
dentro (de)	inside
la derecha	the right
desaparecer*	to disappear
descifrar	to decipher, to work out
desgraciadamente	unfortunately
desde	from, since
desierto/a	deserted, desert
despacio	slowly
despertar (ie)	to wake up
después	later, then
destruir	to destroy
el desván	attic
el detalle	detail
detenido/a	under arrest
detrás de	behind
devolver (ue)	to bring/take back
el día	day
dibujar	to draw
el dibujo	drawing
difícil	difficult, hard
el dinero	money
la dirección	address, direction
dirigado/a	addressed to
dónde	where
dormir (ue)	to sleep
dos	two
duchar	to shower
el dueño	owner
durante	during

E

el edificio	building
él	he
ella	she
ellos/as	they
empezar (ie)	to begin, to start
en	in, at, on
en primer lugar	first of all
en ruinas	ruined, in ruins
encender (ie)	to catch fire
encima de	on, over
encontrar (ue)	to find, to meet
encontrarse (ue)	to be found/situated, to find by chance
enfermo/a	ill, unwell
enfrente de	opposite, in front of
la ensalada	salad
enseñar	to show, to teach
entender (ie)	to understand
entonces	then, so
la entrada	entrance
entrar	to go in, to enter
entre	between, among
enviar	to send
envolver (ue)	to wrap up
equivocado/a	wrong
es	(it) is
el escalón	step
esconder	to hide
la escuela	school
ese/a	that
eso	that
esos/as	those
España	Spain
el esparadrapo	plaster, adhesive bandage
esperar (a)	to wait (for), to hope, to expect
el esquí	skiing
está	(it) is
está bien	(it's) all right
esta mañana	this morning
la estación	the station
el estafador	crook, swindler
están	(they) are
estar*	to be
este/a	this
estos/as	these
esto	this one
el/la estudiante	student
estudiar	to study
el estudio	studio, study
estúpidamente	stupidly
Europa	Europe
exactamente	exactly
examinar	to examine
la excursión	outing, trip
explicar	to explain
explorar	to explore
expulsar	to expel
en extinción	endangered

F

fácil	easy

la falda	skirt	hacer*	to do, to make
falso/a	false	hacer* círculos	to go round in
faltar	to be missing		circles
la familia	family	hacer* compras	to do some shopping
la farmacia	chemist's, pharmacy	hacer* una	to ask a question
favorito/a	favourite	pregunta	
felicitar	to congratulate	el hacha [f]	axe
felizmente	fortunately, happily	hacia	toward, about
fenomenal	brilliant	la hamburguesa	hamburger
feo/a	ugly	hasta	until
el filete	steak	hasta luego	see you later
la fortuna	fortune	hasta pronto	see you soon
la foto	photo	hay	there is/are
la fotocopiadora	photocopier	hay que	you must, one has to
la fresa	strawberry	el helado	ice cream
frío/a	cold	el/la hermano/a	brother/sister
la fuente	fountain	el héroe	hero
fuera (de)	outside (of)	las herramientas	tools
fuerte	loud(ly), strong(ly)	la hierba	grass
el fuerte	fort	el hierro	iron
funcionar	to work, to function	el/la hijo/a	son/daughter
fútbol	football	la historia	story, history
		la hoja	leaf, sheet (of paper)
G		hola	hello
las gafas	glasses	el hombre	man
ganar	to win, to earn	la hora	hour
gastar	to spend (money)	el hotel	hotel
el gato	the cat	hoy	today
gimnasia	gymnastics	el huésped	lodger, boarder
girar	to turn		
el gobernador	governor	**I**	
gordo/a	fat	la idea	idea
la gorra	cap	la iglesia	church
gracias	thank you, thanks	igual	(the) same
grande	big	increíble	incredible
la granja	farm	insistir	to insist
gris	grey	interesante	interesting
gritar	to shout	la intersección	junction
guapo/a	handsome/beautiful (for	ir*	to go
	people, not things)	irse*	to go away, to be off
el/la guardia	policeman/	la isla	island
	policewoman	la izquierda	left
la guerra	war		
la guía	guidebook	**J**	
la guitarra	guitar	el jardín	garden
gustar	to please	el jersey	sweater
		joven	young
H		la joya	jewel
haber	to have	jugar (ue)	to play
había	there was/were	junto a	next to
la habitación	room, bedroom		
el habitante	inhabitant	**K**	
habitualmente	usually, normally	el kilo (de)	kilo (of)
hablar	to talk, to speak		
habrá	there will be	**L**	
hace	ago	ladrar	to bark

Vocabulary list: l - q

el ladrón	burglar, thief
el lago	lake
lanzar	to throw
el lápiz (de colores)	pencil
largo/a	long
lavarse	to wash (oneself)
la leche	milk
leer	to read
lejos de	far from
lento/a	slowly
levantarse	to get up
el libro	book
la lima	nail file
limpio/a	clean
la linterna	torch
lista	ready
llamarse	to be called
la llave	key
llegar	to arrive, to reach, to get
llevar	to carry, to wear, to take, to have
llover (ue)	to rain
lo siento	I'm sorry
lograr	to manage
el loro	parrot
la lugar	place
la lupa	magnifying glass
la luz	light

M

la madera	wood
la madre	mother
la madrugada	early morning (midnight to 5 or 6 a.m.)
el maestro	teacher
el mago	magician
mal	bad, badly
la maleta	suitcase
el maletín	briefcase
malo/a	bad
mamá	Mum, Mom
mañana	tomorrow
la mañana	morning
mañana por la mañana	tomorrow morning
mandar	to order, to send
la mandarina	mandarin
la manzana	apple
el mapa	map
la máquina	machine
el mar	sea
marrón	brown
más	more
el/la/los/las más	the most

mayor	bigger, older
el/la/los/las mayor(es)	the biggest, the oldest
el/la mecánico/a	mechanic
las medias	tights
mejor	better
menor	smaller, younger
el/la/los/las menor(es)	the smallest, the youngest
menos	fewer, less
el mercado	market
el mes	month
la mesa	table
meter	to put in/inside
el metro	underground (railway)
mirar	to look (at)
la misión	task
el/la mismo/a	the same
la mochila	backpack
mojado/a	wet
molestar	to disturb
un momento	one moment, just a minute
la montaña	mountain
el monumento	monument
morir (ue)	to die
mostrar	to show
mover	to move
mucho	a lot, lots, really
mucho/a	a lot of, lots of, many
el muelle	quay, dock
la muerte	death
muerto/a	dead
la mujer	woman
museo	museum
muy	very, really, most

N

nada	nothing
nadie	nobody
la naranja	orange
la nariz	nose
Navidad	Christmas
necesitar	to need
negro/a	black
la nieve	snow
ningún/a	none, no
el/la niño/a	child, boy
no	no, not
no... aún	not... yet
no importa	it doesn't matter
no lo sé	I don't know
no... nada	not... anything
no... nadie	not... anybody
no... ningún/a	not any (at all)
no... nunca	not... ever
no... todavía	not... yet

no... ya	not... any more	pensar (ie)	to think
la noche	evening, night	peor	worse
nosotros/as	we	el/la/los/las peor(es)	the worst
la nota	note	pequeño/a	small, little
Nueva York	New York	perder (ie)	to lose, to miss
nuevo/a	new	perdón	sorry, excuse me
el número	number	perfecto/a	perfect
nunca	never	el periódico	newspaper
		pero	but
O		el perro	dog
o	or	la piedra	stone
ocultar	to hide	la pierna	leg
la oficina de correos, correos	post office	la pieza	piece, room
		el pirata	pirate
ofrecer	to offer	la piscina	swimming pool
el ojo	eye	la pista	clue
oler (hue)	to smell	la planta	plant
olvidarse	to forget	la playa	beach
ordenar	to tidy up	la plaza	square
la oreja	ear	poco	few, little
el oro	gold	poder (ue)	can, may, might
otro/a	other, another (one)	el policía	policeman
		la policía	the police
P		poner*	to put
el padre	father	por	for (because of), through, along
los padres	parents		
pagar	to pay	por allí	that way, over/around there
el país	country		
el paisaje	landscape	por aquí	over here, this way
el pájaro	bird	por desgracia	unfortunately, sadly
el pan	bread	por favor	please
la panadería	baker's	por fin	at last
el panel	panel	por fortuna	luckily
el pantalón	trousers	por qué	why
los pantalones cortos	shorts	por todas partes	everywhere
papá	Dad, Daddy	porque	because
el papel	paper	posible	possible
el par	pair	la postal	postcard
para	for, toward, to	precioso/a	lovely, beautiful
parecer*	to look, to appear	preferir (ie)	to prefer
la pared	wall (indoors)	la pregunta	question
la pareja	couple, pair	preocuparse	to worry
el parque	park	preparado/a	ready, prepared
la parte	part, share	prestar	to lend
pasado/a	last, past	primer, primero/a	first
pasado mañana	the day after tomorrow	primero	first (of all)
pasar	to pass, to spend (time)	la prisa	hurry
el paso de peatones	pedestrian crossing	prismaticos	binoculars
el pastel	cake	probablemente	probably
las patatas fritas	chips, french fries	probar (ue)	to taste, to try
el pedazo	piece, bit	prohibido/a	forbidden
pedir (i)	to order, to ask for	pronto	soon, early
la pelicula	film	próximo/a	next
en peligro de extinción	in danger of extinction	el pueblo	village
		el puente	bridge
peligroso/a	dangerous	la puerta	door
el pelo	hair	el puerto	port

Vocabulary list: q - z

Q

que	who(m), which, than
¡qué!	how!, what!
¿qué?	what?, which?
¡qué bien!	great!
¿qué es eso?	what is that?
¿qué hora es?	what time is it?
¡qué le vamos a hacer!	too bad!
quedar	to remain
querer (ie)	to want, to love
querido (a)	dear
querría	I would like
el queso	cheese
quien(es)	who(m), which
¿quién(es)?	who?
quisiera	I would like
quitar	to remove/take off
quizá(s)	maybe, perhaps

R

rápidamente	quickly
rápido/a	quick, quickly
raro/a	weird, strange, odd, unusual
el rastro	trail
realmente	really
recibir	to receive, to get
recomendar (ie)	to recommend
la recompensa	reward
reconocer*	to recognize
recordar (ue)	to remember
la red	net
regalar	to treat (someone to), to give, to offer
remar	to row
el remo	oar
remoto/a	remote, far away
la remuneración	fee, payment
reparar	to have mended, to fix
repetir (i)	to repeat
el reproductor de CDs	CD player
la respuesta	answer
el restaurante	restaurant
el retrato	portrait
la reunión	meeting
rico/a	rich
el río	river
robar	to steal
el robo	theft
la roca	rock
rocoso/a	rocky
rojo/a	red
romper	to break (something)

la ropa	clothes, clothing
roto/a	broken
el ruido	noise
la ruina	ruin

S

saber*	to know
el sabor	flavour, taste
sacar fotos	to take photos
sagrado/a	sacred
la salchicha	pork sausage
la salida	exit
salir*	to go out, to leave
se busca	wanted
se puede	it is possible to, one/you can
el secreto	secret
seguir (i)	to follow, to carry on, to continue
según	according to
segundo/a	second
seguramente	probably
seguro que	definitely, most probably
el semáforo	traffic lights
la señal	sign
(el) señor (Sr.)	Mr
(la) señora (Sra.)	Mrs
(la) señorita (Srta.)	Miss
sentarse	to sit
sentirse (ie) bien/mal	to feel well/not well
ser*	to be
ser*de noche	to be night-time/dark
servir (i)	to serve
si	if
sí	yes
siempre	always
silencio	quiet, be quiet, silence
simpático/a	nice
sin	without
el sitio	place
la situación	the situation
sobre	above, over, on top of
el sol	sun
solamente	only
soler (ue)	to be used to, to be in the habit of, to usually/normally...
solo/a	alone
la sombra	shade
el sombrero	hat
la sombrilla	parasol
son	(they) are
son las...	it is... (time)
soñar (ue)	to dream
sonreír	to smile
la sopa	soup

la sudadera	sweatshirt	el túnel	tunnel
suficiente	enough	el/la turista	tourist
el supermercado	supermarket	turístico/a	tourist

T

U

tal vez	maybe, perhaps	último/a	last
también	too, also, as well	usted(es)	you (polite)
tampoco	neither		
tan	so	**V**	
tan... como	(just) as... as	la vaca	cow
tarde	late	las vacaciones	holidays, vacations
la tarde	afternoon/evening	vacío/a	empty
el té	(cup of) tea	valer	to cost
el técnico	mechanic, technician	la valla	fence
el tejado	roof	los vaqueros	jeans
el templo	temple	el/la vecino/a	neighbour
la temporada de lluvias	rainy season	la vela	candle
		venga	come on, go on
tener*	to have	vengarse	to get your revenge
el tenis	tennis	venir*	to come
tercero/a	third	vender	to sell
terminarse	to end, to finish	la ventana	window
el tesoro	treasure	ver*	to see
la tía	aunt	verdad	true, right
el tiempo	weather	verde	green
la tienda	shop	vestirse (i)	to dress, to get dressed
la tienda (de campaña)	tent	el veterinario	vet
la tierra	earth, soil, ground	viejo/a	old
tirar	to pull, to throw	visitar	to visit
tirar de	to pull on, to give (something) a pull	vivir	to live
		volver (ue)	to return, to come/get back
la toalla	towel		
tocar	to play	vosotros/as	you
todavía	still	la voz	voice
todavía no	not yet		
todo	everything	**y**	
todo/a	all, every	y	and
todo el mundo	everyone, everybody	ya	already, anymore, yet, that's enough
todo recto	straight ahead	ya basta	
tomar	to take	ya (lo) sé	I know (it)
tomar prestado	to borrow	yo	I
tonto/a	stupid, daft		
torcer (ue)	to turn	**Z**	
la torre	tower	las zapatillas (de deporte)	trainers
trabajar	to work		
traer	to bring	los zapatos	shoes
el traje	suit	el zumo	juice
la trampa	trap		
tranquilo/a	quiet, peaceful, calm		
tras	after		
trater	to try		
la travesía	crossing		
el tren	train		
tres	three		
el trozo	piece, bit		
tú	you		

Usborne Quicklinks

The internet is a great place to continue your language learning. At the Usborne Quicklinks Website, you will find over 80 links to carefully selected websites to help you improve your Spanish. All you need is a computer with an internet connection - then just follow the simple instructions shown below.

Links for Easy Spanish

To visit the recommended websites for this book, go to
www.usborne-quicklinks.com
and enter the keywords
easy spanish

You'll find links to a wide range of websites where you can:

• test yourself with online quizzes, drills and exercises

• listen to pronunciation guides

• use an instant verb conjugator

• look up topics in an online guide to grammar

• find out more about Spain

Downloadable puzzles

There's also a selection of Usborne Spanish picture puzzles to download and print out. You can fill in the puzzles, then go back to the Usborne Quicklinks Website to check your answers. For each picture puzzle, there is a set of clues to help you.

Listening to languages

On many language websites, you can listen to native Spanish speakers. This is a great way to improve your listening skills and pronunciation. Listen carefully, then repeat the words and sentences out loud. You'll feel much more confident next time you have to speak in class, or on a visit to Spain! If you see a loudspeaker symbol on a website make sure you have your speakers turned on so you can hear sound.

Net help

For help using the internet, see the Net Help area on the Usborne Quicklinks Website. There's advice on downloading small, free programs called "plug-ins", which enable your computer to display animations, and tips to help keep your computer safe from viruses.

Site availability

The links at Usborne Quicklinks are regularly reviewed and the websites are updated, but occasionally you may get a message that a site is unavailable. This may be temporary, so try again later, or even the next day.

If any of the recommended sites close down, we will, if possible, replace them with suitable alternatives, so you will always find an up-to-date list of sites at Usborne Quicklinks.

Internet safety

When using the internet, make sure you follow the internet safety guidelines displayed on the Usborne Quicklinks Website.

Please note

Usborne Publishing is not responsible and does not accept liability for the availability or content of any website other than its own, or for any exposure to harmful, offensive, or inaccurate material which may appear on the Web.

We strongly recommend that you keep your computer secure by using anti-virus software and by downloading the free updates for your computer software.

For more information, see the Net Help area on the Quicklinks Website. Usborne Publishing will have no liability for any damage or loss caused by viruses that may be downloaded as a result of browsing the websites it recommends.

125

Index

Acknowledgements

p.12 sunset, car/Digital Vision; **p.13** coastline/Digital Vision; **p.21** teenagers/Digital Vision; **p.25** Gail Mooner/CORBIS; **p.29** women shopping/Digital Vision; **p.33** Owen Franken/CORBIS; **p.37** girls chatting/CORBIS; **p.41** world map, beach scene/Digital Vision; **p.49** skiers/CORBIS; **p.57** Hulton-Deutsch Collection x2/CORBIS; **p.61** Owen Franken/CORBIS; **p.65** boys talking/Digital Vision; **p.69** Fotografica/CORBIS; **p.73** Neil Beer/CORBIS; **p.77** North American Scene/Digital Vision; **p.82** three children/Digital Vision; **p.83** Michael T. Sedan/CORBIS; **p.87** Joseph Sohm/CORBIS and astronaut/Digital Vision; **p.91** Jean-Pierre Lescourret/CORBIS and Michael Prince/CORBIS; **p.95** Stuart Westmorland/CORBIS; **p.124** man with headphones/Powerstock Zefa; **p.125** Kevin Fleming/CORBIS

First published in 2008 by Usborne Publishing Ltd,
83-85 Saffron Hill, London EC1N 8RT, England.
www.usborne.com
Copyright © 2008, 2001, 1992 Usborne Publishing Ltd.

Some of the material in this book was originally published in *Learn Spanish*.

The name Usborne and the devices 🏮 🎈 are Trade Marks of Usborne Publishing Ltd. All rights reserved. No part of this publication may be reproduced, stored in a retrieval system, or transmitted in any form or by any means, electronic, mechanical, photocopying, recording or otherwise, without the prior permission of the publisher.

Printed in Dubai.

Usborne Publishing is not responsible and does not accept liability for the availability or content of any website other than its own, or for any exposure to harmful, offensive, or inaccurate material which may appear on the Web. Usborne Publishing will have no liability for any damage or loss caused by viruses that may be downloaded as a result of browsing the sites it recommends.